A DROP OF WATER

A Spiritual Journey

by
Yvonne Williams Casaus

Disclaimer:

I have tried to recreate events, locales and conversations from my memories of them. In order to maintain their anonymity in some instances I have changed the names of individuals and places, I may have changed some identifying characteristics and details such as physical properties, occupations and places of residence.

Any information within the book is provided and sold with the knowledge that the publisher and author do not offer any legal or other professional advice. In the case of a need for any such expertise consult with the appropriate professional. This book does not contain all information available on the subject. This book has not been created to be specific to any individual's or organizations' situation or needs. Every effort has been made to make this book as accurate as possible. However, there may be typographical and or content errors. Therefore, this book should serve only as a general guide and not as the ultimate source of subject information. This book contains information that might be dated and is intended only to educate and entertain. The author and publisher shall have no liability or responsibility to any person or entity regarding any loss or damage incurred, or alleged to have incurred, directly or indirectly, by the information contained in this book. You hereby agree to be bound by this disclaimer or you may return this book within the guarantee time period for a full refund.

Yvonne Williams Casaus

Laughing At Myself, LLC.

Visit my website at **www.LaughingAtMyself.lol**

Printed in the United States of America

First Printing: September 2016

Published by Laughing At Myself, LLC

ISBN: 978-1-62747-228-9
Ebook ISBN: 978-1-62747-229-6

DEDICATION

This book is dedicated to my amazing children, my wonderful husband, parents, sister, nephew, and one-of-a-kind family and friends. You know who you are. Thank you. I would not be who I am without you.

TABLE OF CONTENTS

PREFACE AND INTRODUCTION

As I have shared with many family and friends, I felt a calling to write this book. As you will see, I never aspired to be an author. I have many roles, a healer, a wife, a mother, a therapist, a sister, a daughter, a friend, but it never occurred to me to be a writer. However, I kept hearing a whisper, a voice in my head telling me I needed to write a book. I have heard it for years, but had no idea where to start. A few years ago my friend told me about a class called "The Artist's Way", based on the book by Julia Cameron. I brought my sister along and we took the class from The University Of New Mexico's Continuing Education Department. I met some amazing people in that class which I still hold dear to my heart. I believe that it opened up the creative juices. It got me to start playing my guitar again, to start painting and drawing again, and to rekindle the voice in my head telling me to write. I started to journal, but would not be consistent with it. I had many attempts at starting a book, but I did not know where to begin. I felt like I was just journaling. In 2015 my dear friend told me about a retreat she was planning to attend by Tom Bird. His, 'Write Your Best Seller in a Weekend' Retreat sounded perfect for someone like me, someone that felt they had a book inside of them. I decided to take a leap of faith and go to a retreat in Santa Fe, New Mexico. I did not know what to expect. In fact, the day before the retreat I remember telling my close friends about it. They asked what the book was going to be about. I remember saying, "I have no idea, for all I know it could be a Vampire, Harry Potter type book". We all had a good laugh, but I really did not know. It ended up being a profound and deep spiritual experience. I wrote from my heart and soul. I wrote about my life, which I had no intention of doing.

During the retreat I had a nice surprise. I had joy in my heart, I had fun! I got into the rhythm of writing and before I knew it I was rhyming! It was pretty shocking and strange to me. I kept laughing at myself during the process. It was so funny to me because I don't rhyme. I love music, I play the *guitar, but I have never rhymed. It was as if my fingers were dancing. I typed with my eyes closed. I was letting the words flow out of my fingertips. I believe that it was God's way of letting me know I was not alone. It was remarkable. Before I knew it, I was sharing my story. Believe me, I am a very private person, I never thought I would share those painful memories. In my heart I know it was God asking me to write it. I have to trust and have faith that this is the book I needed to get out. I wrote it because I was called to and because I believe that sharing it will help others to heal.*

I believe we all have stories to tell, and I say do it! Courage is not the absence of fear. Courage is going ahead and doing what you are called to do in spite of your fear. This book is about my experiences with grief and several tremendous losses. As I rhymed, I became lighthearted, childlike and full of joy. I discovered a connection between water and my spiritual journey to God. It became a fun way to describe how water connects us all. I feel it was spiritually inspired. I hope that in sharing my story I can help those that have ever struggled with depression, grief, or loss of any kind. I hope it becomes a reminder that we are never alone. Water connects us all.

ACKNOWLEDGEMENTS

I wish to personally thank the following people and of course God for their contributions to my inspiration and other help in creating this book: First and foremost my family: My wonderful husband Craig and all our amazing children, Marcus, Thalia, Adrianna, and Zoe. I am grateful for my sister and best friend Kathy, and my handsome nephew Julian for always being there to support me. I would not be who I am without the constant love and support from my mom and dad, Stephanie and Pula. Thank you for all you do. I appreciate you. Thank you to all my angels, living and non-living; mentioned and not mentioned in this book. I appreciate you. I know you have been our safety net. You know who you are. All my precious family and friends that I hold close to my heart. The ones we see at every birthday party, gymnastics competition, and other important family events. The ones that take time every other week or during their lunch to listen and encourage me. Thank you for always being there throughout the years. You have given me so much support through this emotional roller coaster of writing and publishing a book. I am forever grateful to you. I also want to thank each and every one of my clients, past and current. I am honored to be in your life. Thank you for teaching me how to be a better therapist and person in this class called life.

Thank you to Sojourn Publishing for all the guidance and support towards getting this published. I look forward to publishing more books. Last and not least: I beg forgiveness of all those who have been with me over the course of the years and whose names I have failed to mention.

"The most beautiful people
we have known
are those who have
known defeat,
known suffering,
known struggle,
known loss,
and have found their way
out of the depths.
These persons have
an appreciation,
a sensitivity,
and an understanding
of life that fills them
with compassion,
gentleness
and a deep loving concern.
Beautiful people
do not just happen."

*– **Elizabeth Kubler Ross***

DARKNESS LEADS TO LIGHT

We all have dark nights of the soul. I had one of the most heartbreaking moments of all. A moment no wife wants to go through. What I didn't know was that this worst night would lead me to my best life. As dark as this event was, as much as I lost myself, I did not realize at the time that I was making room to embrace the real me. To realize a strength I did not know existed. This is not just my story, it is all our stories. As a therapist, this is what I deal with. I help people embrace the brilliance of the dark nights of our soul. Like a cocoon, it is the necessary preparation for the life they really want. Yes, my story may be more tragic and darker than most, but it also gave me the power and ability to write this book. The harsh fact is I went through the most tragic of all dark circumstances as a wife. The worst night of my life happened on June 5, 2005. My husband, the father of my children, took his own life.

BLACK WIDOW

My first husband killed himself. Ugh. It is so painful to say. It sucks, it still does in so many ways. Most of the time I just live my life. I go through things and know I survived. I really did not want to share the horrible part that brought me here. It makes me feel so vulnerable; now everyone will know. My children do not have their father. My daughter brings it up from time to time. "Why did my dad have to die?" she asks. I wish I had an answer for her. I really do not know; I guess it is just part of our path. It still hurts like hell sometimes — like when the kids have competitions or school functions. He should be there encouraging them, cheering them on. I wish he could share the pride I feel.

I was naïve then, praying and trying to be the best wife I could be. I tried getting him help, I tried. His dad died. He was grieving and instead of feeling, he drank. That was the downfall. He got worse and worse. Once I took all the guns and put them away. He went to counseling and seemed to be better. My dad asked him to go hunting so I gave the guns back. I was finishing my Master's degree in Counseling, and about to graduate. We went to my graduation ceremony; I told him how thankful I was. I remember how handsome he looked in his suit that day. His thick dark brown hair, light brown eyes, perfect cheekbones, and heart-tugging smile. During the ceremony, he was called up on stage so I could give him a plaque thanking him for all his support. He hugged me and told me how proud he was. We went out to eat, and I thought we were good.

Later that night he said he was tired and wanted to rest. Some friends who were moving to Arizona were having a going-away party. He did not want to go so I went alone. I tried to have fun. My friends were leaving for Arizona the next day, so I wanted to spend time with them and say goodbye. He always encouraged me to spend time with my friends. That was something I loved about him. When I was stressed, he would joke and tell me I needed a "girls' night out." He loved to tease, he was also encouraging. He was so kind and so giving, it is such a shock what he did. He was thirty-two years old; how could a man so incredibly smart do something so unbelievably stupid and hurtful to his family and friends?

I loved him so deeply, more than I ever thought possible. From the first time I saw him, my heart skipped a beat. Co-workers would tease me when he would come by my office. I would think, yeah right, he is too good-looking, he wouldn't be interested in me. Pretty soon, Tim, my co-workers and I became really close friends. I remember going to a concert, all of us piled up in his big ancient Jeep. We all had a blast, him running through the parking lot giving one of my friends a piggyback ride. Then later he softly brushed the hair from my face. That's when I knew he had feelings more than friendship. When we were alone together it felt like déjà vu. I was thinking it, and he said it: we have been together before. I knew it was true. I changed my life to be with him. But when Tim looked at me, told me he could see the gold in my eyes, that I looked like an angel, well, there was no other choice.

One night, after I had told him I would call when I got home, I fell asleep and the phone fell off the hook. He got so worried that he could not reach me, he drove across town to my apartment to make sure I was safe. After that night we just stayed together, either his place or mine. We finally just decided to move in together. I loved his son as my own; we traveled, got married, had our daughter. He was so talented and so incredibly smart. We loved to joke that he was a rocket scientist. He worked as a software engineer for Lockheed Martin and the Air Force. That is how we met, I was a satellite engineer, and he taught the class to teach us the software he wrote. He was such a talented musician, he had a beautiful voice. He wrote music and sang hauntingly beautiful songs – but I never realized they were an omen. He was so kind and giving, he would help everyone he could. One of his best friends was a 93-year-old woman. He met her when he was young, he loved to visit with her and every year he put up her Christmas tree and decorations. He loved to help her and spend time with her. She passed away not much longer after he did. I imagine them visiting, talking, and joking around up in heaven.

This is really hard, I cannot stop crying. Oh, Tim, you were such an amazing person, but I still get so furious that you did what you did. You loved your kids. I know you loved me and your family so much. That is what I can never understand. How could you have hurt your family, your friends, your mom, your brother, your kids, in the worst possible way?

If only I had known it would be our last day together. It was early Sunday morning, he was out doing yard work. I went out to see what he was doing. He stopped and we laid on the grass under our tree. I told him about the going-away party, we laughed. My friends invited me to bowling and a movie before they left. He said, "Go, spend time with them, tell them bye for me." I went, he mowed the lawn. Our son went back to his mom. When I got home, Tim was drunk. We fought when he was drunk, nothing new. He went into the bedroom. He closed the door, to sleep, I assumed. I fed my daughter, did our usual routine. But that is not what happened. That was the night my life changed.

Hours went by, and I gave my two-year-old daughter a bath. I was dressing her in her pajamas when we heard the loud bang. I was shocked and stunned. The details are foggy. Was she with me when I finally got in? It still is not clear. It terrifies me that she might have seen what I saw. I could not open the bedroom door, it was locked. I screamed for him to open the door. I tried to open it with a screwdriver and hammer. We had fireplace that connected our living room and bedroom. I got so desperate I climbed through the fireplace, breaking open the glass. When I finally got in the room I saw just what he had done.

His head was hanging from our bed. There was blood on the floor. I still did not get it. I called 911 and held his head. I did CPR just like they said. He was bleeding. I prayed and prayed. I just kept on breathing into his mouth and pushing on his chest. I held a towel to his head, holding in the mess. The gurgling sound did not connect. The door bell rang and I went to get up. Somehow, when I got off the bed, another shot was fired. I opened the front door, and a cop yelled "Get down!"

They thought I shot the gun?! My mind still did not register. Later they would figure it out. I do not remember if I said anything, I just ran to our room. They followed me, saw the scene and sent me out. I sat on the couch. The tears started pouring. One of the cops came out of our bedroom, saying, "I am sorry." I knew what he meant; Tim was gone, he was dead. I cried and I screamed. They tried to calm me, for my daughter, they said, so I would not scare her. Paramedics and fireman poured in the house. Two kind cops cleaned me up and settled me down. Some of the cops played with my baby girl, I heard them say peek-a-boo in her room. They used my phone to call my mom. My parents came quickly. I could not speak. I was stunned, I was in shock, no words would come out. I was a zombie. There were firetrucks and ambulances, with lights blazing. We got in my parents' car and went to their house. That much I remember.

A ZOMBIE

There were family and friends that went to my parents' house. I was such a mess. I could not speak. My mom wanted to go with the chaplain to let his mom, Dorothy, know. I held her tight, I could not let her go. I am so sorry Dorothy, I wish I could have been stronger. I know we all suffered, I was too much of a mess to be there for you. She had to be the one to tell his brother, our seven-year-old son, and our son's mom. I was unable to. My words would not work. I could not even walk alone through the house. My cousin Charles comes to mind. He would have to guide me and hold me up when I walked to the bathroom. I was truly a zombie. He held me up when I would pass out. They had smelling salts. They forced me to eat. I have to say I did not want this, I did not want to share this. I did not know this is what this book would be about. Here it is. My raw ugly story. For a long time I convinced myself Tim did not mean to do it. His gun had a quick trigger, I know from it going off when the doorbell rang. At first I thought it hit me, turns out it nearly did; it ricocheted off our gun safe and put another hole in the wall. I could have been killed. I was so focused on him I never even looked at the gun. I tried to tell myself he did it by accident, that he was just cleaning the gun. The fact is he did it. It was ruled a suicide.

The pain. Dammit, the tears, streaming from my eyes. I did not want to write this. Not about me. I thought it would be about something else. Grief does that to you. It makes you blurry. It makes you numb. Sometimes the pain is so intense that it feels as if you can't handle it. I remember crying so hard I would vomit. I tried so hard to be strong. I thought I had to do everything right. I sold the house, I never lived there again. I lived with my parents, then bought a new house. I went to support groups. I went to counseling. I put all the kids in counseling, my seven-year-old son, my two-year-old daughter, even my three-year-old nephew. We went to the Children's Grief Center of New Mexico, except for my daughter; she was too young. I thank God for that place. Going there was truly a blessing. All these children and families with losses could relate with their peers. The grown-ups met as well, and grew through support and healing tears.

Two years later, I still can recall a moment that was so vivid. I was in a small car accident, nothing serious, but after I called the police, I called Tim without thinking. Then the grief came crashing down again. I had forgotten for a moment that he was not here. I still wanted to call him to help me, it was so natural, such a habit. Moments like that can really take your breath away.

Timothy Kee Williams

TURBULENCE

That was just a little part of the path. I was in a whirlwind, a storm. Then calm waters. I had waves of emotion. Turbulence and small moments of peace. Nights up crying in the closet so the kids would not hear me. Reaching, reading every book I could find, trying so hard to "find the answers." Grief is like water, waves of emotion. It comes in ways we cannot grasp.

Now, I understand. These dark, desperate moments were necessary in my journey towards the light. Like the passage from caterpillar to butterfly, I had to surrender to what felt like a lonely transformation. The truth is— I was never alone. I had so much support my pain kept me from seeing. My family, my friends, people I did not even know. I received their prayers, their love, and their energy. Their support was like a safety net. That must have been how we managed to put our shattered pieces back together. Somehow I found just the right counselor, for just the right time. Thank you Ina Krieble, for all you helped me through. She used EMDR (Eye Movement Densensitization and Reprocessing), a therapy treatment used for trauma. It was powerful. It helped me feel stronger, helped my nightmares and my fear of loud noises. I learned to replace the dark thoughts in my head. I was so grateful and amazed at how much it helped that I later got trained in it. Like a stream I was led to this path, to find currents of healing and hope.

We are never alone. That is the message. We are always connected. A drop of water, an ocean of water — they are the same. It's the same with us, even though we forget. We always forget, we think we are alone. But we cannot be alone, we are all connected. Each and every one of us. We sometimes believe we are the only drop in the entire universe. Sure, we flow with the sink or a river sometimes, but mostly we silly humans feel like we are the only ones going through pain. I look at this drop of water on my plastic water bottle. I am this drop of water. I am and always have been supported.

This drop of water is the same as the water in the ocean. It is the water in my house, the water in my cup. It reminds me that there is love and encouragement we choose not to see. I was always loved. You are always loved. You have never been alone, you can never feel alone again. Water always finds its way. It always joins more drops. It travels, into trees, into roots, into dew on the petals. It is the sparkling frost in the morning. It is the soothing rain at night. It soaks into the earth. It puts out fires. It makes grass grow.

Water is life. We are water. It is hard to remember when we are sad or depressed. We feel so lonely or frozen like ice. We get rigid and cold, but even in ice we are connected. We are connected by love. The sun melts you, you drip, or you pour into a glass. You pour into the person, the dog, or the drain. It does not matter. It is one and the same. That is gross, that is disgusting, you think. You don't want to be flushed, but that is life.

Life can push you and swirl you, make you go down the drain. It can melt us and boil us, whether we are ready or not. I am the water, you are the water. I travel through the meadows, the flowers, and farms. I flow through the rivers, to the ocean, to the pine trees, to the fish and the whales. I travel from the polar bears playing to the lizard in the trees.

You know about water. The healing it does. The trauma it heals. It cleans. It cleanses, it washes, it wipes away sweat and tears. It rinses the blood, the poor victims, the dirt, the disease. People in some countries need it so desperately, water they can drink that is not dirty and full of disease.

"I can speak of gut wrenching pain
Of shock, Of disbelief, Of panic.
The loss of love and dreams, And the feeling of
safety.
Of how I believed nothing so horrible
Could ever happen in my life. I can tell you about
My guilt, My shame, My anger.
But, you have been here. You know what I mean.
What can I tell you
That you don't already know.
But, my story is unique,
What I saw, What I did, What I did not do.
It sits inside me. I can feel its darkness. Must I hold
onto it forever? Should I?
All I can tell you is that
Knowing you are here, Knowing you will listen,
Knowing you will share.
I feel less alone. I feel connected.
And I need so desperately to feel connected.
Your presence anchors me
To this world, To this life, To this new reality.
Without you I fear I would float away,
Drifting in agony forever.
So you are here, And I am here.
Hold my broken heart awhile,

And I will hold yours.
Take my hand
And anchor me. And I will anchor you,
And together we will heal."

-SUPPORT *by Darlene Edwards*

A MESS

Back to my journey, I was still such a mess. I was trying so hard to prove I was strong. I went to a workshop in Denver, to be a better counselor. I felt like such a hypocrite then. A counselor whose husband committed suicide, I felt like a joke. The conference was helpful, but also revealing. I grieved that night, I really felt the pain. I was alone in my hotel room. I let myself cry. I cried so much, so hard. I let myself feel the hurt and the pain. I threw up, expelling the "yuck" in my life. It was very healing. It was painful as hell, but I felt like I woke up. I know I was not the mother I wanted to be. I had "checked out." I worried about the kids. I had tried so hard to do my best and be strong. Looking back, I was as strong as I could be. I was dealing with the house, I was only working part time. There was all the debt he left. I had no idea if I would get life insurance or not if it was deemed a suicide. I refused to believe it. Not my husband, father of my children, a man I loved so very much.

There was conflict, of course. Death brings out the worst in people. It was crazy. Yet, looking back, I had so much support through it all: a safety net, if you will. So much love, so much help. People I did not even know prayed for me, supported me, sent me letters of encouragement. They helped me, they truly carried me. My family and friends helped me so much. Somehow we kept going. The world did not stop no matter how much we wanted it to. Friends and family took turns driving me to counseling. They helped me have garage sales, we fixed the house. We sold it and moved to my parents. We moved things to storage. We all went to counseling and lots of support groups. I did everything thing I thought I was supposed to. I wanted a rule book, a guide book; of course there was no such thing.

I tried to distract myself. I tried to focus on being a good counselor. I tried to distract myself with my career, but it did not work. I do not remember the first year very well. The first holidays are a blur. The second Christmas was much harder. I bought a new Christmas tree, but refused to use anything red or green. It's so funny now that I look back — the way I grieved. That was how I coped. I could not use any old ornaments. We bought new ones, pink, purple, and blue. I started seeing Craig, who turned out to be my current husband. I thought he was the answer. I knew we were meant to be together, but the timing was wrong. I relied on him too much. I was not ready, I was still deep in my grief. I tried to lean on him to give me my purpose, my value, my worth. He could not, of course. No one can. Only through spirit, your higher power, through God, you can call it what you like. I call it God.

Our family had more loss. My nephew's father and my sister's love of her life was killed tragically by a drunk driver. Believe me, we do not take it lightly that both our children lost their fathers at a young age. But, that is her story to tell. One day she will write a book and you can hear how she had to learn to cope and be the most amazing mother, sister, daughter, aunt, and Godmother that ever lived. This of course brought on more agonizing grief and sadness. I learned that any time we suffer a loss, it can bring up past losses. Because I was struggling with it and was so deep in my grief, Craig and I broke up. It did a number on me. I was heartbroken, a mess. I kept waiting for him to show up at my door. I knew I was supposed to be with him. I waited. When it did not happen in my time frame, I distracted myself with another relationship. What a mess that created.

I have always tried so hard to be my best. I have always felt like I had to prove myself, my worthiness. I tried to have a family; I tried so hard. I met someone else and got married again. He loved family, he wanted to coach and referee soccer games. He wanted to be a dad to my kids, or so I thought. He asked my daughter to call him dad anyway. But in the end he didn't stay. It led me to the next chapter. What can I say? It was not the best, but in the end I learned from it.

LORI'S ANGEL DAY

It was Thanksgiving. My sister, my angel, my dear cousin, Lori, died on Thanksgiving morning. It was so heartbreaking, so devastating. It broke me. She was only 32. She died in a car crash, so tragic. Lori was famous for her delicious pumpkin rolls, she had orders from people all over town. She had been making deliveries all day into late in the evening. She was driving the Chimayo, New Mexico curvy Route 76. She drove it all the time so it is still unclear how an accident so tragic could have happened. Somehow she crashed into a tree, and was killed instantly. She was not under the influence, we were told maybe an animal ran in front of her or she bent down to answer the phone or text, we will never know.

It was about 4:00 am when my aunt called to let me know. It did not register, I did not believe her. She said, "I'm sorry, Lori was in an accident, she didn't make it." "What?" I said. "No she wasn't, I just saw her." She had to repeat it several times, I did not want to believe it. My mind refused to let it register. Finally it sank in. She asked me to call my mom, dad and sister to let them know. I remember vomiting violently after I got off the phone with her. Somehow I managed to tell my husband and call my mom. I vaguely remember her saying they would be right there. I got in the shower and bawled my eyes out. It was just so unfair, I remember thinking we can't even pray for her to get better. We can't even go to a hospital.

I got ready as fast as I could. We drove an hour and a half from Albuquerque to Chimayo, New Mexico, where my family is from. It was so unfair, she was so young. I had to be with my aunt Bernie — her mom — and my cousins. My sister Kathy and I were so close to Lori that we considered her our sister. Several years ago Kathy gave each of us a "Sisters" ring, with three hearts; each heart had one of our birthstones. We have all worn them for years, I still wear mine everyday. She was buried with hers. My heart aches. Sometimes it is still so hard to believe she is gone. I needed to be with my family. I had to be there, like they were there for me. There was nowhere else I could possibly be.

I stayed in Chimayo a few days to help with what I could. When the funeral home was ready my sister Kathy, Lori's best friend and I took her clothes and got her ready for the viewing. I never thought I would be able to do something like that. However, it was somehow healing to be able to do something for her. I knew she would have hated the way the mortician did her makeup. I told my sister and her friend, "We better fix her makeup or she will come back and kill us." As painful as it was, we all did her makeup and hair the way she liked, and I polished her nails. I remember she was wearing her Sisters ring. I must have been holding my breath because at one point I got faint. It was hard, but it was nice to be able to do that for her. Now she looked more like our beautiful Lori Ann. She had a beautiful Catholic and Christian service, the local *penitentes* chanted the Spanish Rosary in hauntingly beautiful song. The *penitentes* are a Catholic brotherhood that sing ancient Spanish hymns. When they sing, you can feel it in your soul. As the candles flickered, you could feel the thick sorrowful energy in the room. It was spiritual and powerful. The tears would not stop flowing. Then a Pastor spoke and they displayed the slide show we created. I felt shattered again as I relived the memories appearing on the screen. "How could this be," I wanted to scream "why her?!" She had such a bright future ahead. It was as though our family was shattered, a huge piece was missing. I remember telling my aunt, "we have a unique family, we are one-of-a-kind, and we will get through this". We have all tried to pick up the pieces. Over the years we have tried our best. As you can imagine, Thanksgiving is a rough holiday for us. We all miss her so much. We always light a candle to hold her place in spirit.

What words can possibly describe my precious Lori Ann? The best I can do is talk about her contagious giggle and loving heart. Her laugh could make anyone laugh. She had gorgeous long, curly black hair. She had big, beautiful, dark brown eyes, and long thick eye lashes. She had the most beautiful, heartwarming smile. Her smiling round cheeks and smiling eyes could make anyone feel comfortable and right at home. Thinking of her makes me miss her so much, I start to tear up. I want to lie down and bawl, I miss her so much.

We always had so much fun together. I could always be myself around her. I did not have to be or do anything, or play a role, I was just me. We grew up together, we played with Barbie dolls together and spent summers together. When we got older we would go out dancing together and tell each other everything. She was an amazing barista. She could make a latte with the most amazing designs. She was going back to school to get her degree. She studied so hard. It is so painful to talk about her right now. It is like a piece of me is gone. We have an old video of her from a trip to Disneyland; I watch it over and over to hear her voice and her catching giggle. It makes me smile, and helps my heart from aching so much. She will always be my friend, family and sister in this life and the next.

A FROG IN BOILING WATER

How do you boil a frog? You do not just throw it in boiling water or it would jump out. You slowly turn up the heat so it does not notice it is boiling. That was me; before I knew it, I was boiling.

When I left for Chimayo on Thanksgiving morning, my husband at the time was so angry and hateful. He was mad that I wanted to stay with my family in Chimayo, that I did not want to have a football party. He said he could not understand how I could "bail" on the Thanksgiving party he had planned. He couldn't understand?! He still had a party, had his family over and watched football. I was so hurt. He knew Lori, he claimed he loved her. Yet he was furious that I "chose" my "family" over him. He should have been with me, supporting me, and my family in our loss. That is when I knew I had made a huge mistake. In fact, the day we married I knew, yet I did it anyway. I convinced myself things were good, but I was miserable with him. I lived with constant anxiety. I hoped I would have another child, but he did not want more so I told myself I did not want more. In my heart, however, I knew I did. I cannot believe I got used to living that way.

I kept myself contained, in my own jail cell if you will. But on Super Bowl Sunday, after my mom had surgery, I chose to stay with her. He of course wanted to go to a party. I decided I did not care if he got mad. I was tired of doing things to avoid his rage. I told him I was going to stay with my mom. He got so unbelievably crazy that he broke things, he screamed, he threatened to hurt me.

What really woke me up was that he scared my daughter. She was pleading for help. She tried to call my sister, and you could see the fear in her face. I could not believe I had put her in that situation. What had I done? That is what made me wake up and leave. We jumped out of the boiling water.

We left the house and stayed with my parents. Incredibly, I still gave him chances. We tried couples' counseling. He did not like the first counselor we tried. The second counselor fired us after our first session. She suggested he try the addiction program they offered, as well as AA (Alcoholics Anonymous), and Al-Anon (The Alcoholics Anonymous support group for loved ones) for me. He was not interested so I went to counseling by myself. He told me he was going to AA meetings and like a fool believed him. Then I discovered he was being unfaithful. That's what finally did it, like a switch had been flipped. The proof of his infidelity helped me finally leave for good. It was a shock, I never expected that from him. It turned out he been cheating more than I ever could have imagined. It still makes me sick. The final straw was the woman from his work. He would never admit it, he continued to deny it while looking me straight in the eyes. I was appalled to discover he lied so easily. It used to hurt so much, to feel so betrayed. I never thought I would be the frog. I used that metaphor for clients at work. Yet here I was; a frog in boiling water.

Looking back, I see how it happened. He started out so loving, so adventurous, so generous. He coached my daughter's soccer team. He seemed fun. I was tired of being sad. He took me on trips. We went to Oregon and Florida, even Disneyworld. Of course it seemed good. We moved in together. We got along, we only fought about the dog. Then he started drinking.

When I first met him he was sober. He never drank. The first time I saw him drink it scared me that he could drink so much. I should have realized that his drinking was a red flag, but I did not trust myself. I had lived with an alcoholic. I thought I was just scared. Well, it got worse and worse, he got meaner. We fought more. When we bought a house with a pool, at times it was fun and amazing, at times we were happy. We did family things, and I really liked our blended family. Other times I was miserable and felt like crap, thinking that was the best I deserved.

I do remember feeling so happy when we got our pool. I thought I had made the right choice moving forward with him. I remember lying face up in the water one night. I floated, looking up at the stars, thanking God. It was such an amazing feeling. It was such a rush. But, things got worse.

The alcohol took over, it made him meaner. I adapted; I got used to it.

It is beyond my understanding that I allowed myself to live that way. But after all that effort, I did not want to let it go. I loved his kids, the family we created. He encouraged me to start my own Counseling practice, for that I am grateful. I just kept pretending to the world, my family, friends and clients that I was fine. I presented well, I acted like things were good, that I was good. When in fact I was miserable. I tried many things, I thought I could heal through Counseling, through Shamanism, Yoga, and Acupuncture. In the end I had no choice but to leave. We were not married very long. It was part of my journey. I had to learn to love myself. Sometimes if we are not open to the lesson, it must get our attention through pain. It was another example of how the brilliance of the darkness leads us to the radiance of life. It led me back to my current husband, Craig. I am so grateful for him. His gorgeous green eyes touch me deep in my soul. I know we were meant for each other. I used to feel broken, with him I feel whole. I love our family, his family, his daughters, born in my heart. He is such a good loving man, father, son, brother, and friend. He supports me in ways I could have never imagined. I would not be doing this without him encouraging me. Thank you my love, thank you my family. Believe me, I know I am so very blessed.

"After awhile you learn the subtle difference
 between holding a hand and sharing a life
You learn that love doesn't mean possession,
 company doesn't mean security
And loneliness is universal

You learn that kisses aren't contracts and presents
 aren't promises
And you begin to accept your defeats with your
 head up and your eyes open
With the grace of a woman, not the grief of a child

You learn to build your hopes on today
As the future has a way of falling apart mid-flight
And tomorrow's ground can be too uncertain for
 plans
Yet each step taken in a new direction creates a
 path toward the promise of a brighter dawn.
You learn that even sunshine burns if you get too
 much
So you plant your own garden and nourish your
 own soul
Instead of waiting for someone to bring you flowers

You learn that love, true love always has joys and
  sorrows
Seems ever present, yet is never quite the same
Becoming more than love and less than love
So difficult to define

And you learn that through it all that you really
  can endure
That you really are strong, that you do have value
And you learn and grow, with every goodbye
You learn"

__Comes the Dawn__ *by Joy Whitman*

THE BLESSING

I used to get messages from Craig once in awhile. Little advertisements for the airline he worked for. One day I got one and took a chance. I replied and said hello. From there it sparked a conversation. Before I knew it we were talking non-stop. He asked me to lunch, I was hesitant. I thought do I want to do this again? I was scared. Then I surrendered. Who was I kidding? My heart had been waiting for this. I decided I am jumping in whether I get hurt or not. My mind said don't do it, my heart said you must. Frankly I had no choice, like I always have, I followed my heart. We met at Dion's, a local Pizza place, and it was like we were never apart. We connected again, we dated again. I got butterflies again. We now cherish every moment together and spend our life making up for lost time. He supports me more than I could have ever imagined. He sees me in a way that I cannot see myself. He has faith in me, encourages me, he goes out of his way to give me things I would never get for myself. He gives me courage. With him by my side I feel like I can accomplish anything. He understands how close I am to my family. He is not jealous of it; he is close to his family too. He appreciates how lucky and blessed we are, how much support we have. He has a strong relationship with God. We both have a deep spiritual connection to our faith that makes our love stronger.

When we started dating again, we went on a trip to Washington State. Although I knew I had never stopped loving him, it was this trip that felt like almost a blessing from above. We drove from Bremerton to Port Townsend, Washington. We held hands and walked down the shore, listening to the peaceful water. We walked up to the old lighthouse, Point Wilson and climbed up on the rocks. We cuddled and watched the waves crash onto the rocks. With the warm sun on our face we enjoyed the breathtaking view. It was then we saw the fin of a majestic orca. I had never seen a whale in the wild. It was truly magical. It was God, it was a blessing. This is right, this is good, I thought and felt in my soul. We will have a loving life together.

We do belong together. We can have a strong and beautiful family together. At first it seemed too good to be true. I had not been divorced from my not so loving relationship for very long. I struggled to trust it. The following year he proposed and I was excited yet terrified. I was not ready. He was patient, he waited. I took my time to make sure it was right. I prayed I meditated. It was my ego, my fear that kept me from moving forward. Now when I look back I wonder what I was so scared of. I love our family. When I am in his arms I feel like I am back home where I belong. We have such a fun loving home full of laughter and hope.

Point Wilson Lighthouse, Port Townsend, Washington

Glimpse of a wild orca, in Port Townsend, Washington

"Our deepest fear is not that we are inadequate. Our deepest fear is that we are powerful beyond measure. It is our light, not our darkness, that most frightens us. We ask ourselves, 'Who am I to be brilliant, gorgeous, talented, fabulous?' Actually, who are you not to be? You are a child of God. Your playing small does not serve the world. There is nothing enlightened about shrinking so that other people won't feel insecure around you. We are all meant to shine, as children do. We were born to make manifest the glory of God that is within us. It's not just in some of us; it's in everyone. And as we let our own light shine, we unconsciously give other people permission to do the same. As we are liberated from our own fear, our presence automatically liberates others."

— Marianne Williamson, A Return to Love: Reflections on the Principles of "A Course in Miracles"

MY STORY, NASA

I started my story when Tim died, but before that I lived and did so much. I do love adventure. I know I try to be humble and keep it on the downlow. I have to remember what Marianne Williamson wrote. Shrinking who you are only hurts you. Shine! Radiate! Glow! I too have to remind myself, I am a child of God. I can be who God meant me to be. Yes, I am God's instrument, Spirit's tool, but my humanness has a lot to share too. I can share the glory of God within, to make God's love stronger, brighter and easier to receive.

This life has been exciting, my loving husband points out. I have skydived, worked on space shuttles, scuba dived, and snorkeled with sharks. What can I say, sometimes I forget. I get into my daily routine, trying to heal each person in my office. Why I chose trauma as my focus, I don't know. I guess I mostly can handle it. I can listen to tragic and traumatic stories, then help people to heal and grow. Sometimes it is very hard. Sometimes it feels like too much to handle. Sometimes I feel burned out —as if I have nothing left to give. It is not true of course, it is never ending. It is God. God heals others through me. I am the vessel. This book is going to help, of course. It is about healing your trauma, right from the source. All of us have had some form of trauma, from medical to mental to physical to loneliness. From bullying to feeling all alone. We all get hurt in some way or another.

You are my child, just as you love your own children with their own personalities. They each have their own journey. Just as you enjoy watching them grow, I enjoy watching you grow. You are my child, yes, this was a calling to write, but it is you. You have the message, you are the one, just be you. Your highest self is ready to go. You see it all. You see it. You are beautiful, amazing, brilliant and radiant. You are driven and so incredibly smart.

Why is it so hard to say these things and really believe it, really let it in? We choose not to let ourselves shine. We do not believe we deserve to.

God wants us to. God wants us to shine and be who we are. He wants us to feel our feelings. Just like the movie "Home." When they feel an emotion they turn that color. God wants us to turn purple, red, green, and blue. God wants us to feel and radiate and truly live. To live in the moment, not in the past.

My husband Craig once again reminds me how driven I am. He tells me to remember that I have had quite a life. I went to college, I got really good grades. I worked at NASA. I worked for JPL, but honestly I was not happy. I just went through the motions. Sky diving in Florida, that was freeing. It was a chance to have an incredible adrenaline rush. The air was rushing in my mouth so fast I could not even get a scream out. The powerful wind blowing around me, I felt so alive, so energetic, and so free. I loved it. I loved the descent, the view of the water, even the landing.

Later that August, a hurricane scared me. I saw the power of water firsthand. I was terrified seeing the fierce commanding rain, seeing palm trees bent nearly in half. We went to a coworker's house inland. The scary part was all the glass windows they had. I did not sleep a wink. I just kept waiting and expecting the glass to shatter on me. Then, when it was over, there was no electricity. We had to take showers by candlelight and hang out at Ron Jon's Surf Shop to get out of the heat and humidity. It was so hard to believe, but I could not wait to get home. I missed the brown. I learned to appreciate and love the brown earth of New Mexico, the beautiful Land of Enchantment.

I tried hard to be an engineer. I was smart, I could figure things out, but it did not suit me. The best part about it was the people I met. We had so much fun, my friends and I. We made the best of it. We got so close some of us became lifetime friends. We had juggling contests, played jokes on each other. We laughed at the crazy stuff people did. We made the best of it. I got so much attention, for the first time I felt beautiful. That is when I met my first husband Tim. He came up to me and introduced himself and shook my hand. I remember thinking, "Wow he's cute." Our lives changed. Our love was amazing. He was so smart and so kind. We both worked as engineers. I was a satellite engineer, he was a software engineer. We loved to travel and do things with our kids. Tim loved to build little rocket ships and remote control monster trucks with our son. We would go out and drive them on the dirt. He was always singing silly made-up songs to the kids. We spent weekends at soccer games and loved to travel. One of our favorite trips was going to Daytona Beach and playing with the kids in the ocean. We spent time with our families. He would go hunting with my dad. He loved being a father and a musician. It never crossed my mind that Tim would do something like commit suicide.

I really I had no idea he was capable of such a thing. I knew he was drinking and really a wreck. He was grieving, he had lost his father. He was in pain with knee surgeries and shingles. He kept missing work. I had just finished my master's degree in Counseling. I had my graduation ceremony the day before he died. Instead of the graduation party we had planned, we had his funeral. I will always remember that sunny Sunday morning. The beautiful blue sky, the light breeze, the sound of the rustling leaves. We both were lying on the grass talking and laughing. I wish I had known that would be our last day together. The shock of it still gets me. Now I see him so much in my son. He looks so much like Tim, even sounds like him now. My daughter has his eyebrows, sometimes even his mannerisms. It is so strange. Sometimes I hear his voice so clearly in my son. It can throw me off, and at times take my breath away. It still takes me by surprise.

We have made a new family of our own. My late husband Tim's family, his ex-wife's family, and I have tried to do our best. I am so grateful for all of them. They have always embraced us and included us. My daughter considers her brother's sisters hers, too. I think it is amazing how far we have come. We made it through. His mom is also such a blessing in my life. She helps so much. His brother used to always make time to play with the kids, now he is in China teaching English, his calling. I have so much support, so much love. I just have to let it in. People do come into our path for a reason. They teach us lessons. They help us overcome things. They help us get over our fears. Even my ex. He hurt me deeply, but he did encourage me to start my own practice. To be honest, I probably would not have been brave enough to do it without his motivation. So thank you. Thank you all my aunts, uncles, cousins and friends. I am so blessed with such loving people in my life. My handsome son, he is so intelligent, courageous, and bold. My beautiful, creative daughter, she is so kind, loving and brave. I thank God every day for putting them in my life. At times they are what kept me going, tethered to this world. They teach me and guide me, push me to be better. I am so grateful for Craig, my loving supportive husband, my drummer, my runner. When he came into my life it felt like the missing piece in the puzzle. I felt whole again. He lifts me up and encourages me to fly. I love him so much, I know we are soul mates who will meet over and over again. I love his daughters, my daughters, born in my heart. My oldest daughter, she is so clever, so caring, thoughtful and smart. She too is an author, watch out. My youngest daughter, well she is full of spirit and fire, with hair to match. I am so lucky I get to do little things again. Braid her hair, volunteer in her class, laugh at funny things she says. Thank you my sister, my best friend and confidant. You are my rock. My nephew, he is a true gentleman, growing into an incredible young man. Of course, my Mom and Dad, without your love and support I would not be me. We are so close, this tight family bond is what makes us unique. I would not have come as far as I have. They have gotten me through so many hard times. They have moved me, stayed with me, comforted me, and encouraged me. I am so lucky to have them as my family. I am so very grateful. I feel so supported. That is why I can write, that is why this book is possible.

We had to learn how to live when all we wanted was for the world to stop. I had to learn to take things one hour at a time. My emotions could range from laughing to crying, to being angry, to being numb. I had to learn how to laugh again without feeling guilty. Everyone grieves differently. We used counseling and the Children's Grief Center of New Mexico. We learned different ways to cope. When the kids were little we used to send up balloons to their dad in heaven. We have written letters to him and to Lori. One time for Lori's birthday on a beautiful fall day, all those who loved her, held hands, and gathered around her grave. We had all written letters and planned to send them up to heaven with balloons. There was no helium to be found in the entire area. We decided to burn the letters so the ashes could go up to her in heaven. As we were burning the letters, tears in our eyes, holding hands in a circle, my little cousin said so sweetly, "Where are the marshmallows?" We all laughed and knew Lori would have loved that. It was such a wonderful moment. There was a breeze that went by and I just knew that was her way of telling us she was there, watching over all of us. I now believe that she is like the sun, she can be with all of us whenever we need her.

We learned a lot of things from the Children's Grief Center of New Mexico on how to handle grief. It helped normalized things, and helped us know the emotions we were experiencing were part of the healing. We learned to light candles for parties and holidays to represent our loved ones so it was as if they were there. We eat their favorite foods on their birthdays or we still send up balloons. For Christmas one year, we wrapped a beautiful box and had everyone write down a favorite memory of Lori, then we opened it later and it was such a gift.

Tim always said he wanted to be cremated and part of the earth. On the fifth anniversary of his angel day we poured his ashes into the river. It felt so right and so peaceful. A beautiful butterfly landed right on my daughter's head. I knew it was a sign from him. At different moments throughout the years there have been what I believe are signs from my loved ones. A butterfly will appear during a season there should be none, one of Tim's or Lori's favorite songs will play. Sometimes I can see the most beautiful ray of sunshine from the clouds that could only be my friend Raylah. I am so grateful for these gifts.

It has now been over a decade that my children have had to live without their father. It has been a struggle at times. We have all battled with our grief in our own way. As my kids have grown they have learned to deal with it differently through each developmental stage. We have all been in counseling at different times throughout the years. Sometimes things come up and we need someone outside our family to help us process it. We have gone back to the Children's Grief Center of New Mexico. When my daughter was eleven years old she asked to go there. It helped tremendously. It was and still is a blessing and a safe haven for us to know we can always go back if we need to. I believe it was being with her peers and knowing she was not alone that helped. I never expected it to help me as much as it did. We have had so much love and support throughout the years from so many people, I really feel we have been carried in love. That is what helped all of us heal. For that I am and will always be eternally grateful.

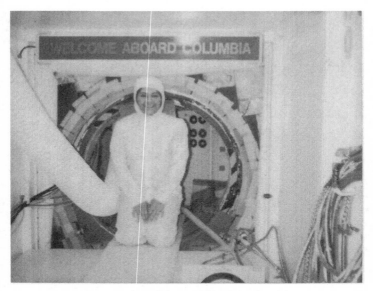

Yvonne aboard Space Shuttle Columbia,
NASA Kennedy Space Center

TRANSITION

This is a warning, things are about to change. As I mentioned in the preface, what I experienced in the process of writing this book was what I can only explain as the spiritual inspiration of God. I started rhyming and had such a joyful, blissful time doing it. I have since learned that people refer to this as "stream of consciousness" writing and that it can be difficult to follow. I was LITERALLY writing with my eyes closed. I found it fun, but here is the disclaimer suggested by my editor that it is about to get silly, playful and spiritually inspired. I for one am grateful that God chose me to let these words flow. That is how I knew that I was exactly where I needed to be. I would never have written something like this on my own. As I kept saying and laughing to myself as I was rhyming, I don't rhyme. All I can say is that it had to be spiritually inspired and God wanted me to have fun while I was writing this. So hold on to your seatbelts! I hope you enjoy it as much as I enjoyed writing it.

THE VESSEL

Yes, it has been a roller-coaster ride. My journey, the pain, it was real. Yet it does not define me, it is just part of the story. I have witnessed it as a therapist as much as I have experienced it in life.

What feels dark and dismal at the time is an opportunity for greater growth. It brought me here, to this very moment. The message is clear. I am here for a reason, to get this lesson out. I wanted this book to be meaningful and healing. I am a drop of water. The dark moments in my journey helped me to appreciate and embrace the beauty and power within. Like water flowing, at times I got stuck in the darkness. My negative thoughts clogged my passage. Finding my way out of the murky water helped me discover the real me. I am the drop and I am the ocean. We are one.

Trust it, just go and go. This is more than you know. You are the vessel. Yes, it is time. Yes, worldly gifts will come. But, it is more, it is timeless, it is heavenly, it is universal. We are about to discover more life. There must be more planets, more galaxies with water and life. This knowledge will help us all to know we are one. From the tree to the table, from the pen to the sun. Now I'm cold; first warm, now a chill. The change in temperature, the goose bumps, this message is powerful.

I am you. You are me. I am God, you are God, don't you see? I am love. You are love. We are all connected. It won't stop, life just keeps going, your friends from this world, from your last, from heaven. There are so many possibilities. Just go with it. It is pouring out of you, remember it is flowing. Just keep your eyes closed, it is better that way. It comes out easier, helps you hear what I have to say. Thank you, my divine author within. Thank you for reminding me I am a divine being. I am me. I am Divine. I am Love, I am Light. With wings and fairies we fly. The message is coming to you; just let it flow. It is not the book you imagined, but who knows. It could be more than you ever thought possible. Just let the words pour out, they are part of the stream.

Water, a drink of water. I just took a drink of water. I feel connected, closer to God, so amazing, look at all the water. Water can swiftly change direction. It can start as a dribble, a tiny drop, it can lead to a powerful force. It pushes, it cleanses, it pushes whatever it wants out of the way. It is a force to be reckoned with. It truly is. It is a powerful force. I see waves crashing down. A huge wave of water can crash and knock you down into the sand. It can knock the breath out of you if you aren't ready. Sometimes it can knock you down even when you think you are ready. It can be frightening and overwhelming, as if you will never escape. You gasp for air and it throws you down again. The more you resist, the more it knocks you down. If you stop trying so hard to control it and just swim through it and accept it, you will find peace. You can discover you float. You do not even have to work so hard, it supports you. Think of the magical ocean creatures, the dolphins and whales. No wonder I love sharks, I see turtles migrating through the sea. Water adjusts, it can wreak havoc or feed and nurture the land.

Love is water. Water is love, pouring out of you one drop at a time. It goes faster and faster, flowing with time. It is timeless really; just keep it going. It is so odd, I never thought of water this way. I thought this would be a novel, or teen romance. Just trust me, just go with it. Water, the love of water. I love water. I am water. You are water. We are water. Water is love.

It is amazing, remember? Recall as a child wanting to run in the rain. Bring to mind how it felt to run through lawn sprinklers or jump in a pool. Water is so healing. You are made of water. Scientists say that the average adult human body is 50-65 percent water. As babies we are approximately 75 - 80 percent water. Who knows how much, really? The food we eat, that has water too. I could go on forever about the connection. We all need water, every single thing on this planet. Open your heart. Open your soul. Even if you are anti-religious, you can trust we are all connected; even if using the word God does not work for you. Call it your divine spirit, your higher power, the

Universe, your best and highest self, whatever you want to call it.

I used to use the analogy of electricity. We cannot see it, but we know it is there and we know it works. We can actually see water. We can feel water. We can drink it and absorb it. We can soak in it. If it is something you can see, it is something you can believe. God, your higher power, your spirit is water.

Water is nourishing, you know that to be true. Now you can see we are all connected. There is no fighting it. You are never alone. We are never alone. It is okay to feel your feelings. Just feel them. It will change, it will go where it needs to. It is okay, it is safe. Let it heal you. Have faith. Just trust it. Go back to being that precious child. Have fun, blow bubbles, play in the tub. Dance and sing in the shower. Remember, relearn how to have fun. Play! Scream at the top your lungs under water. It is safe. It is exciting!

Just keep going, don't let it stop. It's like a block, my left brain, trying to control. It's okay, just go with it. Remember I am in you, I am you, the words just pour out. Don't think so hard just let it out. I trust in you, you trust in me. I am God, you are me. These are my words you hear pouring out of your soul. Don't put up blocks just let it flow. You are doing just fine do not judge it. I know it is not what you thought. Just let it go, a novel with love triangles and vampires it's not. You had an inkling this would be about healing. Well, here it is, more powerful than you think. This is the message. We are connected. Water connects us all.

JUMP IN

As a child I would jump in so careless and free. Just feeling alive, refreshed, so very happy. I am so relaxed, so blissful, so grateful, so pure. There is no worry, no fear, just float and endear. Like a seal, I flow and can jump through the air. So amazing, so awesome, without a care!

I am grateful to you and grateful you see, for this is an amazing and precious opportunity. I am releasing it, letting it go. I don't know how, stop judging it, just let it flow. Close your eyes so you won't keep trying to fix it. This is for you. This is for me, it is for all of us, you see. If it is healing for you, it is healing for me. For her, for him, for even this bird. For all of it, every bit of it, just let it go. I am so happy so let it out. What fun! I just want to shout!

I'm writing; I'm rhyming! So funny. I just can't believe it. Keep it going and flowing don't stop.

This book is going to heal, don't worry. Just go with it, flow with it. Just tell the story. I was swimming with dolphins and whales and fish. I jumped out of the water, scared the birds and the fish. I am a shark swimming with grace. Then a turtle living in space. I jump onto a boat and travel quite far. To Kenya, to Australia, to Italy, why not? There are so many paths and adventures to try. Everyone is part of the journey, there are millions of souls just in this body. They are all encouraging and praying and leading you on. This drop of water travels and travels. It goes on and connects. Sees all its pals.

I can't get over this rhyming, it's a trip. Just go with it, love, it is fine you are a drip. I am so funny! I can't believe it. So crazy I know, but it is true. We are water, we are everything. We are truly one. It is true we are here for a journey. For a swim. I jump in the water, I taste the salt. I feel the warm water. I blow air out. I jump in the ocean, swim with the fish. Feel it like it is here. I am here. I am everywhere. I am in the air, in the earth, I am the fire, I am the metal.

Jump in the water. Hop in, feel alive, feel your body move. It flows. Jump, swim, kick, scream, dance. It feels so good to be alive. It is energizing, rejuvenating, powerful, the sound can be so peaceful. The sound of the rushing water in Jemez Springs, New Mexico, or the sound of rain dripping, the drops pounding the rooftop. The sound of waves, so soothing and relaxing, or scary and terrifying.

Jump in with the dolphins or the beautiful fish. The warm water. The taste. Warm and soothing, comforting, cold and refreshing. Lukewarm, washing your hands, get clean. Let it flow, let it release. Get it out, flush it out, flush it away. We love water parks. Having fun sliding, jumping, jumping in waves. The cold water at first did not feel safe. It was shocking and jarring, but I loved the beach. I loved the waves, so fun, the lazy river at our old water park. That is so funny, I hear Lori laughing. I hear Tim joking about the fluoride in the water. What we choose to absorb, what we choose to feel. Alone or together. Connected or disconnected. Opposite to water, there is no opposite. It is fire, earth, metal, air. Hmm, the fire.

The fire inside me, the drive. Working together. Wow, warm, cold, clean, dirty, back to love. God. God is water, the Holy Spirit. We bless ourselves with Holy Water. We get baptized with water. Rebirth, love. It makes us whole, it fills us up. It is energy. Fluid dynamics. It flows and drips and moves with what appears random energy, but it is not. It collects, it changes. Like love changes. If I love water so much, was I a sea creature? Possibly we were all sea creatures.

MY LOVE OF WATER

My love of water. I love water. That explains my affinity to swimming pools. What about people who are afraid of water? Are they are afraid of love? They have been hurt by water. They jumped in, got overwhelmed, perhaps nearly drowned. It can be scary, we can drown ourselves in the process of love. We can lose who we are, become what they are. Adapt, flow only when needed. Have the confidence to come together. To balance, to be at peace. Balance, feel the waves coming, flowing, the roundness. Ride the wave, do not let it knock you down. It looks like the edge of the world. It is not, it is the never-ending cycle. The flow, it never stops. It comes in, comes out, we are not alone in a glass. We are still connected. We still come together. Whether through a tree, a tiger, a pair of spiky heels. It never stops finding its way back home. From darkness to light, from pain to healing. We must endure the heartbreaking dark nights of the soul. It helps us prepare and adjust to the unexpected brightness ahead.

Water. It is universal. We are all looking, searching, finding water. We all want to feel connected and whole. We start as a drop of water drawn to the whole. Searching, connecting. Some take certain paths, some flow in giant waves, some make food, some nourish, some clean. We find each other. We heal in relationship. Water heals. It changes, it has many journeys. It can be together in a wave, a tsunami, a sprinkler feeding the grass. It can be reaching, connecting, dripping, flowing, cleansing. Water, release it. Release, flow out of me. Cleanse me, get me connected. Bring me home.

My road always leads me to water. I feel it, then I separate into a tiny drop in the bottom of a glass. I join the rest in a cup or sink. Then I go up and separate. I can be steam and flow back into the air to be absorbed by the earth. Flow into a cloud, or a beautiful snowflake. I can land on a car, or melt on someone's tongue. Then back into the little girl playing on the pier. Jumping off into the wholesome, warm place, feeling alive again.

Taste. Tasting the salty water, then rinsing with clean water. The warmth of the shower on my hair, my face, truly peaceful. Joyful. The joy of water. The love of water. A water gun, a water fight, splashing, not worrying about the color of my hair, being truly free and peaceful. So grateful life is unfolding fast it should. It is flowing. I stepped in and entered the flow. I am not going to hold on to a branch or climb out soggy out of fear of the unknown. I am going to trust the process, trust the flow of life. Let the water take me where I need to go. Let it flow. Enjoy the ride. Sometimes exhilarating and fun. Sometimes peaceful and tranquil, soothing and relaxing, so grateful for it. So happy. Joy, radiate joy. Let it flow.

I jump off a pier and splash into the water. I feel so alive, so refreshed, frankly so loved. It is healing, it is true. I find my way to you. Keep going, like Julia Cameron, in her book "Finding Water." My divining rod lead me to this. It is inside of us, in every ounce of us. In the sink, in the drink, it is everywhere. We are on the path. We can make our own path. We can be a little drop that makes its way into the ocean.

ANGELS SINGING WITH JOY

I am writing from the heart, my soul is writing what I now know is God. My soul wanted this story told. I hear God and my angels singing with joy. They are having such fun, laughing with delight. They are so proud, I cannot believe it. It is finally time to get the message, get it out with rhyme. With rhyme you say, are you crazy, is this a joke? How could this be? A book with the rhythm of song. I do love to dance. I love Zumba and Salsa and even romance. Seriously, I cannot believe it. I feel I should get serious and start really doing this. This is it. This is the book. This is God. I am God. Just let it out; God wants you to sing, to dance, and to shout. Enjoy it, have fun, laugh if you like. My angels are so happy. They cannot stop flowing and glowing. Are you kidding? Oh my, I am ready, to write the book you would like, just help me get the words out.

Just keep going. It is just flowing out of you. I am holding your hand. My darling sister Lori, I see your curls, I hear your giggle. Thank you so much for being with me today. My friend Raylah gives me a deep loving hug. I miss you my friend. I keep seeing you. These are the words I hear them say, "You are confident and kind, you have so much to say. The world will benefit from it. I value your worth. You know what you are doing. You know how to heal, to get people to listen. When you speak people really hear what you have to say. They let it sink in. This book will help people let it sink in. This will help so many more than you know."

Raylah was always so supportive, it's her voice I hear in my head, "I see Oprah talking about it, you can feel it. People will benefit from it. They will feel peace. They will feel calmer, they will feel love. They will want to color. Children will enjoy the sing-song of the words. It is awesome." Oh my dear angels, thank you, you make my heart smile. Thank you for that. I am so glad I could know you.

Oh my dear friend Raylah, you are with me every day. She too was a healer, a mother, a friend. Raylah Etlantus was an amazing counselor, she helped so many. She always believed in me, made me feel valuable and worthy. She died from cancer so quickly, so unexpectedly. She had just started her own Counseling practice; she loved the counseling technique EMDR (Eye Movement Desensitization and Reprocessing). We worked together, took walks together, I respected her so much. I later moved into her old office suite. It is where I run my private practice. It is so perfect for me in so many ways. I feel her with me, hear her confidence in me, everyday I use the beautiful chime she gave me.

My angels keep singing and lifting me up. I am the eagle flying above. I see the earth, I see all the water. I see how we are all connected. My angels embrace me, fill me with love. This is so amazing. I am so grateful. Yes, telling this story is part of what my soul came to do. There are still more adventures waiting for you. Of course there will still be bumps in the road. It is just part of the journey, the adventure of life.

Raylah Etlantus

AGUA

Drink it, feel it, let it flow. Water, water, water? Hmm so strange, what is the word in other countries? Agua, Eau, Wasser, Shui, Vodda, Vatn, Acqua, Vann, Woda, Vatten, Su, Water, more ways to say it than I can name. We are free. We can soar like the owl and eagle above. See the reflection, see the hope, so beautiful, so calming. I am so grateful for where it begins.

A drop of water. A single drop, ready to flow. We start small, clinging like the baby in utero. Just the same as the water in our home, we get in it, submerge in it, feel and expand.

We are all the same — the water, the crystal, the ice — we are one. Heal, destroy, rage, whatever you decide. The choice is yours. You know it in your brain, your heart your lungs, your gut. It is all water, all blood. It is all Jesus and Buddha, the Dalai Lama, all the same. Practice kindness, be loving, be gentle, be humble, be brave. It is all those things. It is time, so just go with it. Enjoy it and flow. I love it. I am getting it out. We are. I am. This is. We are connected. We are one.

We are not alone. Anyone can heal from it, in any language. We all know the language of water. We all experience water, we all feel it. That is why this works. We know water and how it can help us heal. Think of the language of water. It shifts; it transforms. It can help us grow and change, but most of all feel. We have all experienced water, each and every one of us has felt it, drunk it, cleaned with it. We can use it to help us heal, and feel.

THE LANGUAGE OF WATER

Water is sacred, it is powerful. It is energy, it is love. It is purified. It is salty, dirty, cold or hot. It boils like anger, then simmers. We need it to live. We cannot survive without it. We are water, we are love. I am water, flowing, setting boundaries. Thinking I am separate, but really everything is connected. The sink, the cup, the plastic water bottle. The glass, the plant, the soil, all of it. Just let it flow and know that I am. God is in you, God is in me. I am love. Love is me. You are me, I am you. I am love. Love is water. Water is love.

We think we are disconnected and separate, but we are all one. We are all together. We are all love. Feel the love, feel it inside. Let it flow, just feel it. Drink some water. Feel it go down. It is energy, it is healing. It is love. We all need it; some of us crave it.

I love water, I always have. What about those who fear it? I wonder what they fear? Is it the love, the closeness, the togetherness. We are really connected, whether we believe it or not. We are water, we are love. From the one tiny drop. I imagine jumping in and feeling alive. Splashing and playing, so safe, so fun.

Emotion, the language of water. Water is a metaphor for our emotions. My emotions have felt like a hurricane or pot of boiling water. Sometimes I feel like sprinkles, or a giant wave pool. My emotions crash, rise, and slam down. Sometimes I am the dew on the leaf. I just sit peacefully and serene. I take my time, then decide to drop down into the grass. Water is a language, a way to feel. A way to explain our emotions.

Water is healing. Water is pain. It can be cold or hotter than hell. It can burn you or freeze you, drown you or clean you. It is as mean as a shark, a tiger, or a bear. It is the white polar bear jumping from the ice to the freezing cold water. It is the icebergs and water from deep down below. I just have to remember it is part of the plan. It is part of the journey. Just keep going. It is telling you, remember to have fun. To live the life you dream. To live more than you can dream. It is more than you can imagine. It is amazing, wonderful, kind, and peaceful. It is Joy. It is Hope. It is Faith. It is Love.

As a Play therapist, I often see the metaphor of water as emotion. When a child dumps a whole bucket of water in the sand, it can be a big clue as to how they are feeling. Are they flooded with emotions, do they feel out of control? When they want water and put it in the sand very slowly and calculated, that too, is a clue they feel out of control. They want to mold it, manage it, they try so hard to control it. Then they try to wash it off, or flood it. Was it too scary to go there? A flood of emotion or an attempt to wash away the feelings?

I know I have cried in the shower. The water helped me release the tears, the profound pain I was carrying. There were times I flat out bawled like a baby in the shower. At times it was the only place I could cry. The water brought the devastating heartache and agonizing emptiness to the surface. I was afraid to scare my kids or my family. I could see the fear and helplessness in their eyes when they would see me in pain. Sometimes I still cry and do not know why or where it is coming from. It is just part of the release, part of the transformation. They are healing tears. Looking back, those tragedies were a catalyst, forcing me to grow in ways I never thought possible. They helped to unleash my inner strength and embrace the real me. Transformation never ends. Like water, it recycles. We must learn to accept the ups and downs as we do the infinity symbol. It is simply part of the process.

We hear, "We are all connected." We say it, but do we truly believe it? We often feel disconnected and isolated. We stay in our own little bottles of water, like Oprah Winfrey says, in our own cups of water. We think we are alone, we tell ourselves we are different, we think, "We are not part of that ocean." But we are. We are always together. We are always connected. We are the trees, the rain, the air, the breeze. It is far out there, I know. Just go with it.

TAKE A SIP

Imagine it. Take a sip. Drink warm water. Let it soak in, feel it go down, nice and warm. Jump into a pool. Do not worry. Feel free. Float. Water is earth. The earth is water. How strange, but it is true. I keep seeing a whale, a smile in its eyes, saying, "I know you, I have seen you before. You can do this. Let the words flow." Am I water? Am I the journey, the connection?

Drink the water, drink the tea, eat the food made of water. Sit at the table that was made by water. Drink it. Wash with it, clean. It is powerful. What if we thought about it as love? What if it is love? What if we let ourselves feel just how loved we all are, how connected we are all. Think of the endless possibilities. To believe, truly believe, we are connected. We are love, we are one. The drop clinging to the cup, changing and transforming, until it once again becomes the ocean. That is the process. The journey is the process, the adventure. Enjoy the process. Embrace the adventure.

Come with me. I love you, love me. Let it flow out, let the words go, just let it be. I am grateful for this opportunity to let you all know what water can do. It is holy. It can heal, it can love. It is more than enough. It is blessed. We are blessed. What if we truly believed water is love? We are made of water. That would mean every time we touch it or drink it we could feel loved. We could feel blessed.

We are all part of the cycle. Even if we think we are separate for a little while, we are not. These drops, this cup, they are still made of water. They are God. I am you, you are me. Oh how I wish you could see. This is it, let it flow. Water is a powerful force, you know. I know a part of you still thinks it is crazy. How funny, how silly, just go with it, baby.

My "Aha moment," Oprah would say. She is my dear friend, she is yours too. That is why you know this is true. I love it. I love it! Woo hoo! Whew! Wow! I can't believe it, but it's true. Come on left brain, stop correcting it. Just let it go, let it flow, let it go. Of course this is true you know it.

Go go go go don't stop. This will be a book you say? Of course. It is from me. I am God, you are God. We are the same water.

SEARCHING FOR GOD

I have always loved water, always felt a calling to it. My soul is drawn to it. It was always my way of finding God. Finding water, finding God. As a young adult I was called to move close to it. I wanted so much to live by the beach. I did internships at NASA Kennedy Space Center in Florida. Then NASA JPL (Jet Propulsion Laboratory) in California. I loved the ocean. I loved the beach. Yet, I never got in, not all the way, not until I snorkeled. My first time snorkeling was in Key West, Florida. I was so impressed, the warm water was so clear and turquoise blue. I had so much fun there, I sky dived, I went on road trips. I was used to the brown earth of New Mexico. Somehow despite all the fun and the beautiful greenery, I missed the brown, the Land of Enchantment.

I think as a child I played in the ocean, in California with my parents. However, it was not until my first vacation with my first husband Tim that I really got in. That is where I felt God so strongly. We went to Florida and I jumped in all the way. We swam in the warm Atlantic water. We swam together past the crashing waves to the deep part. We just floated and enjoyed it. I looked up at the sky and saw the sun. I looked at the horizon, what looked like the end of the world. The way it drops off. No wonder they thought the world was flat. I let myself open up and really feel it. I mean really feel and be connected to the water. I felt God. I truly felt God. More than I had ever felt God before. I felt it. I am it. The spirit inside me. It was so peaceful and serene. Frankly, so fun. I had always liked water as a child. I loved to swim. My favorite was to swim facing up. Seeing the sky and the sun all distorted. I felt so free, so uninhibited.

We jumped on the waves. We went scuba diving and snorkeling; it was so amazing. Like I said that is when I really FELT God. It was an incredible feeling. So peaceful. I felt so whole, so complete. It is a feeling I always crave. I always want to go back to that feeling. As I was floating in the warm ocean water I looked up at the sky. I felt God's presence so strongly. I felt so loved, so peaceful. It is so hard to get that feeling. I have tried. I have gone to churches and Adoration Chapels. I prayed for guidance in these small, sacred places of worship. An Adoration Chapel is a place to pray and be in the presence of the Eucharist, the Catholic Blessed Sacrament. Those places were peaceful, but merely scratched the surface compared to the warm, loving embrace of the ocean. Perhaps I felt God's love so strongly in the water because I could feel the connection. We are connected through water. I felt the tender affection on my skin and peace in my heart. I heard the soothing sound of the waves and the seagulls calling out in the wind. Like a baby in utero I felt safe and secure. I felt it completely and entirely, with all my being. After Tim died I was so lost. I was so angry and sad. I thought God had left me. I yearned for his love, that feeling of support. I tried so hard to find it, to find peace. Like I said, I went to churches and Adoration chapels alone. I went to our favorite parks. I prayed and prayed, the way I knew how. I was asked recently if prayer has changed for me. It has. I was raised Catholic with a routine of prayers. I always said them in order. Perhaps it was the grief after Tim died, but I could not feel Spirit. I was numb. I was angry. I tried for years. Until one day I went to a service and the tears would not stop. I let the love in. I am the one who had cut off my umbilical cord to God.

I could not get back to the feeling I had in the ocean. It was when I was deep in the water that I truly felt the presence and love of God. When I really let it in. Maybe that is why I let it in. I let myself be silly and goofy and just let myself feel it, really feel it. I still pray. I still sometimes pray my prayers in order. It helps, but what comes to me was a conversation I once had with one of my clients. She said she did not know how to pray. She said someone told her she could sing the ABC's and God would know what she was praying for. God already knows. It is already in your heart. Just pray. Just say the ABC's if that is all you know. I am sure there is a water prayer and I just do not know it. That is okay. It will come. All I can share is what I know.

There was a time I can recall now. I was with Craig, years before we were married. He is very spiritual, I went with him to the church he attended, I was still angry with God at the time. I had a hard time letting God in after Tim died. I have to admit, I was a mess. I was so angry, so sad, frankly depressed. Anyway, we went to Craig's church, and it hit, I felt it. I let God in, the tears would not stop. They just kept flowing. No matter how hard I tried, the tears kept pouring out. I ran out of tissues. I could not stop crying. I felt God in my heart. I feel it now. Breathe it into your body. Really feel it. Feel your heart. Let the energy in. Let the light shine in. Let it come in through your head. Keep letting it flow through you.

The thing is, God was always there, always loving me. The love never stopped. Just like my own children. I do not stop loving them just because they are mad at me. I always love them. God is patient and kind. I feel God now. I ask for help. I ask for guidance. Every day I ask for help, help to heal my clients. I ask, "Let me know the right words to say." I already use God's word to heal. Now I can help so many more. Really let yourself feel these words. Feel them. Say them.

I am love. Say it. I am love. Drink some water. Feel it go down. Feel the love. Feel it. Feel the connection. I feel it. I feel you. If nothing else know that I, Yvonne, love you. I love you and always will. I am just a human, but I believe that I feel God's love. I believe that I hear God's words and use them to help others. I have faith that God uses me and my experience to spread the message. In my practice I believe I am just the instrument that helps my clients heal. I hear the message now.

WATER IS LIFE

Water. Water is life. Water is love. Water can dance. I think of the Bellagio in Las Vegas, with their dancing fountains. They sway and jump with the music. I hear the fountain flowing in the spa room next door. It is so peaceful, so serene, hard to ignore. How good it feels on my skin. I feel it, the water, the water within. My soul is yearning for a refreshing cool drink. I long for the ocean, to swim under water. I desire to travel with the sparkling fish, the wise friendly turtle, and the mystical mermaid deep in the sea. It is so magical, so meaningful, so emotional too. It is crazy to write about water, I know. Yet, I feel happy. I feel peaceful. I feel grateful and loved. It is wonderful. I feel so blissful and ready. I feel the divine author within, just writing what comes. I am just writing what is flowing through. I am writing with my eyes closed, it is God writing, not me, not you. My love, my dear, my spirit, my soul, just let the words flow out. Just let them go.

I have always been drawn to water. I feel at peace, whole, closer to God. I think of how it feels to jump in cold water. The shock that comes over you. The aliveness of your senses. It wakes me up. It makes my skin tingle, it makes me feel so alive. It reminds me to wake up. As an adult it is so freeing with a childlike sense of wonder to imagine jumping in the water without a care. To play! I love it. I will be more mindful of it. I will notice how refreshing it feels in the shower, how soothing and comforting it feels in the bath. It is the sweet nectar of life.

I see the little girl inside me jumping in, feeling free. I see her doing cartwheels in the grass of my neighbor, Mrs. Watt's, yard. So care-free, so joyful. I am excited. I am so happy! I cannot wait to sit on Oprah's chair, visiting and sharing. I laugh, but I feel it can happen. The energy is flowing so strongly. The message is so strong, the message is coming.

I AM LOVE

Water is life. Water is love. I am love. I do not just love others or feel love from others, I am Love. It is a hard concept. It was hard for me. It finally clicked one day, during a Yoga workshop. We had to ask ourselves, what is the message your soul wants you to hear? I got the message loud and clear. I AM LOVE.

It was not to feel love, receive love, it was I AM LOVE. So I am asking you to feel it, feel the water, feel the love. Like water, I get stagnant, I get dirty, then clean. I transform. I change, I ebb and flow. I start in one direction then go completely another. I drip or cause damage, create peace or cause fear. I can come out a mountain, and drain out of a house in less than a year.

Here comes more rhyming. Take a deep breath and relax, just let it stream. Trust it, just go with it, go with God, and know. I am water. You are water, too. I know it seems like a crazy concept to you. Just think about it. We start on a path then we go different directions — sometimes following the stream, sometimes making our own way. We end up in so many places to name. From the jungle, to the restaurant, to the ones playing their games. We really truly are all the same.

ONE DROP OF WATER

Imagine the journey of one drop of water. She emerged from the ocean, from the clouds and the rain. She traveled through icebergs, lakes and streams. She just did not remember. She decided to take a journey. Where should it begin? It is never-ending. She thought life was over, but it was just a new beginning. A transformation. A new adventure.

Like any soul, she thought she was all alone. She started as a drop, forgetting she was just in the ocean. All she could see was the edge of the cup. She clung to the edge, then dripped down, not knowing where to go. She fell in a stream full of fish, they said, "There you are, we missed you, have fun." She slid into a crevice and soaked into a root. She traveled through the soil, through the trees, then splashed down and got stepped on by little bluebirds.

She helped grow some leaves and blossom a flower. She flew out a sprinkler, down the street into the drain. That part was yucky and scary. She did not like it at all. She went through the darkness, searching for light, hoping to come out the other side. She got through the dark tunnel and went into the sky. Some graceful birds, then an eagle flies by. She turned into a cloud and rained down below, into a lake full of children ready to go. They were laughing and splashing and screaming with joy. She jumps off a pier into the water, fresh and clear. It feels so alive and invigorating. She jumps and screams and loves it for the taking. She stayed on the hair of a cute little boy. She jumped back and forth between his little friends, then clung to his skin on his way home. When he showered she went down the drain. She traveled some more not sure where to go. She just kept being carried and went with the flow.

There is no beginning or ending just where you want the story to begin. That's the point, it is never-ending. It starts as a drop. It flows and goes. It is happening as we speak. It is peaceful and wonderful, healing and warm. We can feel it, we can see it. It can cleanse, nourish, awaken, and push out toxins. It can support, heal, the same as love. What a comparison. Water: you can trust it to be an unknown powerful force to be reckoned with, a nourishing force. It is like love. Love can be so freeing, so peaceful. Water loves unconditionally. It flows unconditionally. It drips when tightened, flows, supports, it nourishes. It is. Water is love, it reacts, it feels, it rages. It does not mean to. It just is. It is never-ending. It can flood, it can grow crops. It can carry bacteria. Hmm ... is there dirty love? Water can carry pain, it can destroy over time, or with one flash flood. It can flow, it can overflow. It can do so much. Without it we cannot live. Just like love. We cannot live without love.

We are love, I am love. I am made of water. Therefore, water is love. What an idea. A powerful one. Water is love? What about people terrified of water? Are they afraid of love? We all must learn to love ourselves. What about the other elements? Fire, air, earth, metal all part of the miraculous transformation. It is Alchemy. It is energy, it is love. The energy of water is no different than that of the Phoenix rising from the ashes. Rebirth, recycle. It is never-ending, always in movement and changing states, from liquid to vapor to ice and back again. The ocean turns into vapor and emerges as clouds. It releases the rain, sleet, hail, or snow. It nourishes the earth and maintains the oceans. Then it condenses into clouds and starts the cycle all over again.

When I was young I often felt scared and shy. I definitely did not want to shine. I just wanted to hide. I did not want to be seen, and I do not know what I was afraid of. I know I loved water. I loved bath time, I loved swimming. I loved to splash. I loved to run in the sprinklers. When we got a pool it was so magical. It was an above-ground round pool, and it was like we hit the jackpot. I loved it so much. I felt so free in the water. No boundaries. I did not have to play a role, I could just dive in. My sister and I would make water shows like the old movies. We would twirl, and do flips, and swim upside down. I did love to see the world a different way.

It was so fascinating to look up at the sky from underneath the water. Swimming under the water face up toward the sun reminded me of feeling connected. That is why I loved it so much. I thought it was because I wanted to be a mermaid. Swimming was my heaven. It could be so peaceful, so freeing and joyful for me. My cousins would come, and my sister and I would have so much fun swimming with them. We would play in the water all day. We would jump and scream and make waves. We would get out to eat and then want to go right back in. I have never given my love of water much thought until now. I knew I was drawn to water, but I thought it was because of my astrological sign of Cancer, one of the water signs. It makes so much sense now, it almost seems too obvious. How did we not think of this before? Perhaps someone has and I just did not pay attention. It is possible.

Sometimes, I am like the drop clinging to the top of the water bottle. I do not want to believe in something until it is right in my face. I think, I am just a little drop of water. I believe I could never be part of the ocean or the stream. Yet we are one and the same. You are both, you are all of it. I am the stream, I am the ocean, I am this drop in my water bottle. I am the water inside me.

I realize some people are frightened of the water. Some are scared to swim, but I know you have had water to drink. I know you have cleaned yourself with water. It is not something to be feared. It is you, inside you, inside me, it is you, it is me. I know I am repeating myself, but it is true. We are not alone. Not at all. I am in my children, my husband, my clients. I am in the couch in my office. I am in the bell, the toys, the wind chime, the lights. I am in this mocha, this chocolate.

EMOTIONS

It is just a way to explain. Water is everything. In this bottle, this cup, in the lemon, the orange, the honey, the cough drop. My left brain keeps stopping this music from flowing. Do not worry my dear, just release it. Remember, I am you. I am writing through you. Thank you for listening. Thank you for going, for coming and doing what I ask of you. The words will come out, just let it happen, don't hesitate, don't slow. It is okay, just go with it. I know it feels almost wrong, just listen, just trust it. I am God, you are me. I am water and the tree. I am everywhere. I am here, I am there, I am the air. We are never alone, not even in a cup. I made the cup, I am the cup. It is just what you see in this world. This journey you chose to foresee. You asked friends to join you, to help you learn. They said okay and came for some fun. You did love them all. You had a great time. You danced and sang and slid and giggled. Thank you, Lori.

Thank you, Tim. Thank you, Raylah. Thank you Mrs. Watt, my grandmotherly neighbor, my "Nana." You were right, I am a teacher. This is it, let it flow like the water, just let it go. It is going and going, it won't stop. I can't believe it, my fingers can't keep up. I am so proud of you my precious child. We are all connected — this is the message. We are love.

What a journey this drop chose to take. You chose to jump into the lake, then join the ocean, a magnificent waterfall. Then travel by shark, so familiar it is all. Your friend the whale says hi and the coyote too. He saw you passing on his way to you. You travel by stream, by a flower in spring, by some torrential rain. I flow out of you. No, but wait yes. I did go to Kenya. I got dirty then clean and came to New Mexico. I am you. You are me. Let it go, let it flow, just let it be. This is it, you are getting it out. Stop judging it, just go with it, do not let it stop.

This drop of water is a mix of all of you, the whole earth inside. It is water. It is me, it is you. It is all of us, it is inside each of us. It has been flowing out of you, out of me. Don't you see, you are me. I am you. We are writing this to see. To help the world flow, to help us all grow, truly know we are linked.

Emotions are just like water, they flow and change. It is true, they are never the same. They can be as cold as ice. Frozen and stiff, and then melt into a drop and seep into a crack. Imagine the water boiling and hot. It burns my mouth, but it is really good stuff. Like the shower this morning. It heals and breathes. It steams up the room and keeps me going. I am so happy, so grateful. Water is everywhere.

It can be volatile, yet serene and amazing. A drop of water. I feel it. Water is everywhere, just like me. I am God. You are me. We are all connected. I love you all, each and every tiny last drop. Sometimes we are rivers, sometimes we stay still. Sometimes we flow, then rush like a flood, ravage and rage. Let it go up the roots of this little sunflower. Let it turn into mini drops of dew. It goes inside like energy, or it drips and cries. It comes out as tears of healing. We are not different, we are all the same. We get cold, we get warm, we adapt and develop. Just like life, the only definite there is. We cannot help it, we must learn to accept it. To embrace and grow.

The quote comes to mind. "The Universe is change, life is what our thoughts make it," by Marcus Aurelius. I have loved that quote since I was a teenager in my Language Arts class. I tried to conjure like magic, the life I thought I should have. I followed the "rules." I did what they said. I went to college, I married, I worked. I tried to be a good mother to my darling stepson. I prayed, for my child in my womb. I prayed for my love to spread far. Like many, I had the irrational belief that trying to be a good person would keep me from harm. As I have learned from my own life and as a therapist, bad things happen to good people. We tend to focus on the injustice instead of the gift. These jarring moments can bring us to awareness and enlighten us to the wonderment of life. In the darkness, we feel lost, shattered and broken. But, these are really moments of grace, of learning and growing. There are always lessons to be learned. Sometimes we receive the lessons easily, sometimes they are painful.

In praying for my love to spread far, I discovered the unlimited abundance of love within me. Who knew I would grow to love so many. I love all my children, the ones born from my womb, or born in my heart. A mother to many, so many children I love and hold. I love all the children that have been in my life, my stepchildren, my cousins, the ones in my practice. These children still have so much to teach me. Like my daughter, an old soul, she helps me learn and grow. She has so much knowledge, not human, but deeper. She has been here before.

OUT OF THE DARKNESS

Is God in water? I would say yes, some would argue, or feel they know what is best. I just know my own experience. I feel God in water. I feel God's love. I feel it deeply. Every drop is a blessing. Do other universes have water and love? Hmm ... good questions. I do not know. I just feel it. Water is love.

It is an early morning; with dew on the leaves. It is a cold brisk day where you can see your breath. Aaah, the fresh crisp morning air. I breathe it in deeply, filling my lungs with the hope of new day. The colorful painted sky, I see the warm sun coming up. The vibrant sunrise is breathtaking. There are purples, pinks, yellows and hues of blue swirling through the clouds. It is so incredibly gorgeous. New Mexico has the most amazing sky. I take in the beauty of the changing leaves on the surrounding trees. It is so peaceful, yet miraculous, all these vivid colors. The rich shades of yellow, orange, and green are so brilliant and inspiring. I wish I could capture this magnificent canvas with paint. I take a picture with my phone, but it does not do it justice. A drop of water drips from a leaf. "What a beautiful morning," I say as we walk up the hill. I point out the beauty surrounding us as we walk to the bus stop. I send my youngest daughter to school, my little red-headed green-eyed beauty. I walk in my house, I get ready for work. I hear a calling, a whisper of sorts. It tells me there is a story inside you. I want you to write. I think, I don't write. I was never a writer. I am not an author, I am a healer. That, I have known for a while. I tried to do left brain, it was not my style. I was unhappy. I had a calling but felt I was in a rut. I went back to school to be a counselor. They thought I was crazy. I completely changed my career. From an engineer to a counselor! Totally different, but I felt it. I felt the calling. It felt right. I loved it, it was where I belonged. I loved the classes, got straight A's; I loved it all. Of course that was until my husband got so sick. I do not mean sick in health, well he was that too, but sick in spirit.

I tried to focus on raising the kids, not being depressed. But there was that one time when I felt so alone. I thought the world would be better without me. What was I thinking? It could have ended right there. No baby, no future. I had lost hope. I could not see a way out. Fast forward to Tim acting paranoid and thinking there were aliens. Walking around the house in fear, making me push the bassinet with our baby, huddled all together because Tim could not be alone. His eyes crazy, drugged, but at the time I was clueless. So naïve, I did not know. He was drinking and using, to an extent that was unbelievable. Not until after he died, when I had to clean his old Jeep out, did I discover the back covered in bottles. I was shocked. How could I have missed this? I was in so much denial. It was dark murky waters, keeping me from seeing and growing.

I see now, God saved me, in that drop of water. From the tub, the shower, the water I drank. God brought me back, out of the darkness. Those dark nights of the soul guided me towards the light of life. God gave me strength when I felt I had none. I felt hope. I kept going to school. I worked full time

and worked on my master's degree. I kept hoping
and praying for the best, for happiness.

I AM WATER, I AM THE TOOL

Oh my child, you work so hard, you care so much. Now it is time for fun, for the needed self care. You tell people to love themselves, yet you work so hard. You help and you heal, you get yourself worn out. You get tired and start feeling doubt. Could this really be? A rhyming book? Just trust it. Just go with it.

What is water? Water is everything. It damages, it cleans, it makes us sick when not clean enough. We say it in school, in our silence. Life class is not what you think. It is more than you imagined. Just let it start with the drop. Let it flow from the bottom, from the bottom to the top. A drip in the sink, a splash from the sea. I feel you. I am you. You are me. It is a reminder, a memento, to remember, we are all in this together.

I am water. A drop in the sea, a drop in the river, a drop in the ocean. A drop feeding the seed.

I am everything, everyone, every piece of the world. So much you could feel if you let it be known. We are all connected. You know it is true. Just let the water flow, you mermaid you. Oh God is this really possible? A book full of rhymes, is this really your gospel? Am I really writing of water in rhythm? Yes my love, yes my child, just feel it. It is love, I am love. Water. Water! Water?! I am actually laughing out loud. I feel so silly, yet so proud. Thank you God for this opportunity. I am the tool just like in my work. When I counsel, I ask for guidance, to know what to say. I help clients heal. I am the vessel, the relationship. We heal in relationship. I am trying to make the connection to that. The words just come out like a stream. The ocean, the waves, just let it drift, again and again. It is okay. Just listen to it, open your heart to it. It is so funny, I am having a blast. I love writing. I love it. I never knew it could be such fun. It is time. It is time to be free. It is so funny. I crack myself up. I never expected this to occur. What a joke I keep thinking, just like Murr. Is this an "Impractical joke?" Murr is one of the jokesters on the show "Impractical Jokers". I laugh at myself. I'm not sure what this is. I can't stop it so just trust it, just go with it. Other people write from the heart. They let it flow and get it all out. I just can't stop. I just want to laugh and leap from the top. That yoga ball is calling, calling my name. I am going to jump on it and laugh, so I can feel it again.

The warmth, the freshness, feeling alive. Yes, it is true. I am alive. Let's do it together. I am you, you are me. We are writing this book. It is so very funny to me. My little brain can't get enough. I cannot wrap my head around it, so strange, so tough. I am God. I am love, you are me. We are all in this together, do you not see? It is happening. It is coming, it is flowing from a single drop. That is the story you are holding.

Oh my, you say how can this be? Am I really writing a poem, a poem? Me?! You cannot be serious! You must be joking. How can I really be writing in rhyme? I am writing from the heart. Just let it pour out. I am going to love myself today. Writing and healing, learning to play. Play with the words. They really are amusing. My polar-bear friend is saying jump in, get in the fun. You know it is flowing out at great speed. Just keep it going, just keep flowing through the water and the seed.

What the heck is going on? I am going nuts. How is this happening? I really do not know. It is just the rhythm, part of the flow. The beat of my heart that sings with joy. To let his book happen, to come into being and be whole. It is a healing message you see. It is time to let it out.

Let this be a healing tool. Let it be more than you can imagine. Let God heal you. Surrender. When you take a drink, notice it. Notice the journey. Then notice the next time you are by or in the ocean. Know I am here. This is me. This is God. I am Love. You are love. Water is love. Even dirty water, is it just afraid? Terrified to be loved, to clean the pain away? Let yourself feel it again. It is fine to go with it. Let it rhyme if you like, have fun with it. Just let it out. Is this a comedy? No. Yes, kind of. The rhyming is funny and crazy as hell. The words are pouring out again, a drop at a time.

I am you, I am God, I am water. I am earth, I am fire, I am air, I am metal. I am all of it. We are connected; remember, do not forget. I love water. I am water. Water loves me. I jump in, feel refreshed, I am covered with love. I love my family, my friends, my loves, my daughters, my sons.

DANCING

Remember the journey. Angels help me stay connected. Help me feel the source. Let it pour a steady flow into the massive ocean. There must be water in other planets in other forms. Let it flow. No pressure, let it drip out if it likes. It is okay. Thank you again Lori, Tim, Raylah, Mrs. Watt. Thank you all my grandparents and guardian angels. Guide me, connect me. This body is tired, but the voice continues. There is a message, a healing message. It will heal more than you know. It is lovely. It is love, it is peace, it is favor. It has the power to reach thousands, possibly millions. My religion is kindness, love, joy, and peace. I believe in the healing power of love. It is so peaceful, to embrace a different view of the world. There is harmony in my heart. Thank you God, I feel you, I am you. I am blessed.

Yes, it is time. The seed was planted, it is sprouting and transforming. The path is shifting, the road is changing. The world is developing, healing, and feeling. We are all children of God. We are growing, we are the connection. Thank you for listening, for being open, for jumping in, for taking the plunge. Thank you my child. I think of my children and how I love watching them grow. Smiling at them with love, as they grow from infant to stubborn three-year-old, then snotty teenager. It is part of the path. Trust it. The first word of the year, Trust. It will work out as it needs to. The details take care of themselves.

The angels sing, your angels praise. I hear them. "You can do it," they say. The smile, the gifts of encouragement. Thank you. We see each other again and again. Become one another, each drop is a soul. Souls all together connected. One decides to become a drop and start a new journey. The adventure, the unknown, the challenges, at the time seems fun. With twists and turns. Are angels water? Is that the left brain? Oh my child, I love the questions you have. It is that spark, the curiosity that makes us unique. Angels, energy, water is energy, angels of water. Is there such a thing? A water angel? The water angel, the magic, fairies and butterflies, spinning and dancing, twirling, up and down. Swimming face up looking at the world differently. It is all together so powerful.

It is amazing and wonderful, my water angel. If I could I love myself the way I love my children. The joy I feel from the questions my soul wants answered. What is the message? I am God. God is flowing out of me. The words are flowing, I am transforming. Breathe. Connect. Release. Thank you my angels, I hear you, this is where I should be. I feel you with me, deep in my heart, you are gently wiping the tears from my eyes.

I feel so much love and support. It is time for the tears of healing to come. The water, the healing water. Liquid from the bottom of my toes to my ankles and knees. My hips and stomach to my chest. My shoulders and arms, my elbows, my hands. The words flow easily. It is easy to let it come out. My fingers are dancing. It is time, my love. It is time, love is powerful. It is time to find the calm, the peace before and after the storm. The storm is part of the journey. It is part of the cycle.

Let the storm rage on. Is this a joke? The cold never bothered me anyway, let it go. Ha, I have seen "Frozen" too many times.

Stop worrying my love, it will be okay, you deserve the joy. Love your husband. Love your children, love everyone. We learn and grow, like Louise Hay, you already know her, you know Oprah, you have been friends before. Even Joel Olsteen, you recognize him, know his energy. It is your turn. Relax. Your very own Aha moment. Of course we all know each other: we are all water, we are everything, we are the same substance. It is time to let your voice out. Let it out now. Let it flow and sing and yell and dance. I love it. I am free. You felt the resistance, but no longer. It is time. I really want to sing, to let it out, scream, laugh, set my voice free.

Yes. I am free to fly, fly so high like angels and butterflies, fly through the heavens, fly through the oceans, and soar through the sky. It is time to take flight. Splatter like waves, leap to the sky. It is time to spray like the whale. You see his smile. He is having fun, the dolphin too. I hear them saying, "I see you." Scream with the seagull, gulp with the shark. Even sharks like to fly and dance, and shoot out of the water. What do fish read? The waves, the flow of energy? The movement. It is time to read the signs, to let the seed grow.

My sister said it, she is one too, everyone you meet, every soul in this room is someone in the great big balloon. What? A balloon, you say? Yes, the water balloon, why not? So fun, I can't seem to get over it. Thank you coyote, I hear you. Yes, I hear you now. Really feel you now. Yes, I will see you again. There is no need for sadness. It is gone, let love in. Let God know, let it ebb, let it flow. Too much fun? No such thing.

Shoot, you are rhyming! Versing and singing, let your voice out. It is the ego trying to keep you from shouting. You felt the calling before. I am the mermaid, with her voice back. I am here. God's story to tell which of course is mine, and all of us, hell! We are all water, not just in the cup, the drop, the drip. I am deaf, I am silly, I am funny. I am smart, I am kind. This book will never leave that behind. It is fine. I am sleepy, a little tired, not weepy. Just letting the music come out of the pen. I love it. I knew it, such Zen.

A drop of water. Here we are a little drop of water. Let it go into another. Let it seep and ripple and grow. Soothing, healing, springing, growing. I hear myself rhyming, see myself flying, dancing, jumping, and singing. I do cartwheels, twirling. We are connected. Water connects us all. It is God, it is the angels. I know there is something trying to keep me from going. Remove it, my Angels, please cut it with your mighty swords. Release it. Cut it open. Aah, a release, I sigh, I breathe. The healing water flows through me, it pours out of me, the words pour out like energy. Start at the bottom and fill me up. Feel it traveling, absorbing, healing, I am the water. I am the lemon. I am the cough drop because I am everything. I am in everything. I am love, I am energy.

I am water. I am. I feel the healing energy of the room. Let it surge out of me with a steady stream. I experience it pour out, it travels, nourishing every crevice. Enriching the body, mind, and spirit. This is it, it is time. It is pouring out of me, into you, filling every hole, completing every cell. Let it swirl, release, and heal. The warmth, the drip. The soothing feeling. I am the body, I am the spirit. I am the water, the energy. Of course I can rhyme without a dime. Have fun. Jump in. Feel refreshed. Feel warm and cozy now, let it go down, so soothing releasing, cleansing, and healing.

Let it flow, write with your eyes closed. Feel me enter your body like the body and blood of Christ. The water of God. I am God, take me in. I am peaceful, warm and soothing, healing. Feel me, feel my love in your heart, in your chest, every cell, every single little drop. Feel it going down. Feel my love, feel me flowing, let it go down, healing your chest. Your lungs, your stomach, it absorbs into everything feel it. I feel it flowing I feel it healing. Let it keep flowing and going, spreading your wings, flying, seeping in, relaxing. So peaceful and wonderful. Relax, heal, feel the nourishment, let it sink in. Let the vitamins support, get it going. Releasing and flowing, keep going do not stop. Let the energy of God keep going and going. Healing the seed that was planted long ago. You know it to be true. I wanted the words to come out of you. It is okay to laugh and joke. Gushing and flowing, so funny I am. Yes indeed, Sam I am. So happy and joyful, the feel of love pouring out of me. What do you know, it is God. It is me. I am you don't you see?

Feel the vibration, the connection, the knowing. We are all souls, connected and growing. I love it, love it, love it. I swear, I'm a poet! A poet it seems. Oh joy, I should have known all along. Feel it, be it, it is strong. Go go go! It is time. It's time for the show. Oh my word— is that the Muppets? I feel nuts. It's another angel, I feel it in my heart, it's my cousin Peter. I hear his hearty laugh. Oh Peter, you could always make me smile.

I hear a voice narrating this poem. It is awesome, so awesome, the way it is flowing. I chuckle, what a hoot. Wait— I recognize that silly laugh. It is Lori's giggle! Thank you love. I hear it, "Hee hee hee ha ha ha, Joyful, joyful, joyful as all." Please let it flow. Please let me sing, do not stop. Just feel it. Feel it within. It is me, it is you, your voice, my voice. I am so happy. You are singing, you are using your voice. You held it for so very long. Time to let it out, this beautiful song. "Aaa aa aaa, aa aa aaa" let it out. Like Ariel, the Little Mermaid. Sing, sing, sing! Let it flow. I am you, you are me. I know it is hilarious, hysterical, and awesome! I can't believe it. I'm rhyming. I love the people, the souls in my life. I feel the joy. They are here, all my angels, what a party! I feel so very blessed, oh my heart is filled with joy to feel and hear you all again. Thank you for being here, for knowing me in this life. I have known you all before of course. I recognize and see you through your soulful eyes.

Now I see my angel Jimmy, my precious little neighbor, so tragic when he died. I hear him giggling and riding on my back. I was ten, maybe eleven when I lost that darling little boy. We used to play with him like a brother, we loved him, our very own little doll. He is another angel. I just felt him, almost like I dreamt him. He is smiling and I know he is here too. He passed when he was not quite two. A tragic accident, he was run over, he ran out, he was little, the driver could not see him. We were told God needed him more than we did.

My daughter, my love, my beautiful girl, the teacher, the guide, more than you know. My husband Craig, of course. I know that in his eyes. It is like looking at water, at love, blue and green skies. Oh my, what a thing, rhyming? Me? Of course my child. I am God, you are me. I am inside you. Inside each of you. All in this pen, this orange, this table, this hall. It is funny you think, the cynical part of you. Trying to stop yourself from believing it's true. Of course it is me, of course it is you. Let it pour out of you. I am you, you are me. Together you see we are one. We are all the same, we are part of the cycle. We think we are separate for a little while, but really this table, this glass, is all made of water.

WE ARE CONNECTED

We are connected whether we believe it or not. We are in this together. We can try to separate, become just one drop, but we always find more. We travel nonlinearly to our next destination. Whether it is a swimming pool, your cup, your shower, the voyage is never-ending. I know it sounds funny. I never thought of it that way. I swim. I drink. I shower every day.

What is water? Is it love? Some people will think, "Not to me." Just try to remember, feel it in your heart. I am love, you are love. You are God, God is me. It is in everything in the world. It is a way to connect. We use it to describe our emotions. So in depth. It can feel separated and very alone. It can be the ocean, never ending. It is waves crashing, a soothing sound. The sound of water is really profound. What is the reason for writing this? To remember, it is true. We are all together in this.

How else can I say it, we are all linked. A drop does not die. It gets absorbed, it transforms. The earth soaks it up. Water transforms and so can we. We can use it to wash away the pain. We do not have to carry it, we can let it flow out. We do not have to hold it in alone. We do not have to say here is my trauma, here in this cup. We hold it and carry it and dirty it up. We think we are damaged and can never be fixed. It is not true. We can do it. We can. Just take the next path. Just go with it. Just keep flowing.

It is the pine cone, the tiny one, the big one, the big pine tree. We are all connected! I just want to cry. I feel it. The sun in my face, the birds singing. The autumn leaves falling. It is so incredibly beautiful. You never have to feel alone. You are not. Look outside. Hold this book. We are connected.

We all have dark and dreary nights. We have all had loss of some kind. I am saddened by the loss of memories of my Grandma Ruby. She died when I was very little, yet I feel the love she had for me. And, despite the sorrow I felt after losing my Grandma Josefina, our time together was a gift forever engrained in my heart. We lost her shortly after little Jimmy died. I vividly remember crying on the drive to Santa Fe to see her in the hospital. It was the day the ambulances were at Jimmy's house, I didn't know who to cry for so I cried for both of them. I am grateful for the memories of love in her warm cozy home. I can still smell beans cooking on the stove and sitting comfortably in her lap while she braided my hair. I can taste the sweet treat she used to give us of Peanut Butter and Syrup in a bowl. My sister, cousins and I would eat this concoction with a spoon. It is still a comfort food for me. I have noticed I crave it whenever I feel stressed. It must by my body's attempt to self soothe, to achieve the safety, comfort and love I felt in her presence. I can only think of such a memory as a gift.

Yes, there is sadness in life, but fun and joy as well. It is a beautiful life. Life is beautiful. Victor Frankl wrote the book "Man's Search for Meaning." He found meaning in the darkest place in humanity. He was a Holocaust survivor. He survived the mass killings of the Jews in the 1930's and 1940's. He found meaning behind the suffering. So what is the meaning? It is part of the journey. It is the next step on the path. From the stream, to the snow, to the river flowing. The meaning of this is we are all ONE. We make it complicated for some reason. It is easy. We are safe. Be humble, be grateful, and be kind to others. Feel the energy. Water is energy, a drop in the ocean. A drink of water from the bottle, the bottle made of water, so many things at once. It is genderless, connected. Pretending to be disconnected. Is it possible? Is it God? Am I water? Yes, I am everywhere, I am everything. I am the bottle, I am the cup. I am the paper, I am the chair, I am all of it.

Life is a journey, never forget. It is time to stop trying so hard to control it. It is uncontrollable, just like a flood. You think you are guiding it, but it goes on the path it creates. Not the path you think it should take.

A drop of water. That is what we think, when we feel all alone. That is not true, we are never alone. We are always connected from the drop, to the sprinklers, to the grass, to the trees. From the stream to the river, flowing, connecting to the ocean. We are the storm brewing. We are the rain, feeding the grass. We never stop. Our souls never stop. We keep finding each other over and over. We are never alone. When you feel loved you feel whole and complete. This is a way to help you remember. This drop of water is the same as the ocean. We are the crashing waves, splattering in the sand. The crab that crawls out from the hole. The same one the child used to make a sand castle. We are the water used to wash the sand off our feet. Then we walk inside and have a drink. This is to remind us to never feel alone. That is the message. We have been and will always be connected. Yes, it is powerful. Really let that sink in. That is a huge relief. To know we are never alone.

When you feel alone, crying in your bed, thinking no one can understand, this book is to remind you, you are never alone. Take a drink. Take a bath or a shower. Feel me. Be me. Know I love you. You are loved. You are love. Say it out loud. I am love. We all try to resist it. Some of you flat out won't believe it. I think of my clients. It is hard to accept. It is hard to let it in. It is scary and vulnerable to open your heart. To allow yourself to feel it, and let it seep in.

Ruby Martinez

Josefina Maestas

WATER IS POWERFUL

Water is powerful; it can be calm and slow, yet strong. It can flow peacefully, yet destroy the road, wear down a path. It can come in a wave and cause a flood. Water heals the world, nurtures it and feeds it. Luckily we adjust and learn to swim. I swim and swim. It can be so much fun. I love to be underwater. I used to want to be a mermaid, flowing, seeing the world, how we are all connected. Truly peaceful and relaxed. Whether warm or fresh or cold. Water is the anger, acidic, alkaline, dirty, clouded, purified and clean. So powerful.

I love the adrenaline rush. I feel so free. I fly through the air. I feel like I can go anywhere. My body just flows. I want a bath, a soothing soak. It refreshes me. A happy laugh. I giggle and scream, no fear. It refreshes me. I see my little cousins jumping in, no fear. I see my daughter jumping and doing cartwheels. Not just finding water, connecting to it. The cycle. Part of life, part of us, part of me. I have always been drawn to it. I do not feel alone in water. I feel connected, closer to God. So amazing, look at all the water. It is God, it is earth. I feel called to write about it.

Oh my here I go again. God help me. What is this? I wanted it to be fiction, a sort of Harry Potter story, with vampires and love. But water? Then the part about me? That is not something I thought I would see. Maybe it is just part of the healing. I am doing it, God. I am writing the book you called me to write. I never thought of myself as an author. I am a healer, a counselor, a play therapist, a mother, a sister, a daughter, a wife. I have plenty of roles. Author never occurred to me. Yet, here I am. Writing your words, in rhyme no less.

THIS IS HEALING

This book is really about healing and not feeling alone. Of course there are so many stories to share. Like when I was so scared of loud noises. They would paralyze me. I would often dissociate or feel disconnected. I would be in a room full of people and feel far away. I have struggled with the dark depths of depression and debilitating anxiety. It was a battle. In the end I had to choose what felt like the harder path. I had no idea that wading through the darkness would lead me to a life I never dreamed of. I had to learn to think differently. I had to be aware and change my old unhelpful thought patterns. I repeated positive affirmations. It was not easy, but I began to believe them and attract good things into my life. Thinking positively is much harder than thinking negatively. It does not come naturally, we are not taught to think this way. Negativity has more energy. It is hard to stay positive. I say that all the time. But— it is a choice. You have to choose. You have to learn to replace the negative voice in your head with good loving thoughts. Put loving thoughts into your water when you drink it. It sounds so simple, yet at first feels so hard to do. If we were to really embrace it, imagine the good it could do. We could heal the earth.

I, too, take water for granted. I shower everyday. If I were more aware and more mindful I would see it and feel it. We are all connected. It is time, in this cup, in this honey and lemon. In the bottle, in my breakfast, in heaven.

My husband, Craig, just came to mind. I see him opening the door for me. When he holds me it feels like anything is possible. I feel so safe and so loved, so inspired and beautiful. He helps me to see myself in a positive way. He is encouraging me to write more about my life. My love of my clients. I do love to help people. I do like seeing them grow and feel more confident. I love the little ones. The children I help heal with play. They have so much to say. We just have to listen to them, speak play. That is their language.

This is a story of healing, of finding my way to God. My journey of finding peace, and ultimately, truly letting joy into my heart. Not just saying it, but really truly embracing it. Radiating joy, and love. The journey really is powerful and amazing.

This is a story of love. I love Louise Hay — anyone who knows me knows I believe in her affirmations. I reference her book, "You Can Heal Your Life," nearly every day. In this book she shares how our negative beliefs and thoughts can affect our bodies. She believes if you change your beliefs, you can prosper. She shares many positive affirmations. I use her book quite often, for myself as well as my clients. Pain is often a way to get our attention. I have found her positive affirmations a useful and easy way to change negative thinking. It is always helpful to reframe our situation.

Our thoughts are powerful. Masuruto Emoto comes to mind. His book "The Hidden Messages in Water," is a profound example of that. He took photographs of ice crystals that demonstrate how words affect the physical structure of water. He found that words could make the molecules shape into snowflake like crystals or jagged rocks. Words such as "thank you" and "I love you," caused beautiful geometrical crystals. Words such as "you make me sick," or "you fool," caused ugly distorted images — some with no crystals at all. If thoughts become things and words affect water, imagine what our thoughts, loving or hateful, do to us.

A DROUGHT

A drought is like not letting yourself feel love. Being desperate for just one drop. When you are feeling lonely that one drop could make all the difference in the world. We feel parched, dried up, not letting the love in. But the truth is we can be in two forms at once. We can be frozen like ice, or melting, boiling, or steaming. We can be rigid and frozen, needing to thaw. We stop moving and get stuck. Or we can defrost and melt our hearts. We can open up to the flow of life. We can start slow or go into a rolling boil. We can boil and get so hot. We burn, we cook things. We make it clean again and pure. Like water we can be powerful, angry, soothing, serene, or quenching and truly amazing.

Feel it now. Open your heart. Feel it grow. Notice it. If you want, you can do this now, it is how I help my clients learn to feel. We are so numb to our bodies. We live in our heads. If you have resistance where do you feel it? And no, not in your head, in your body, from your head down. Notice it, what color is it? Does it have a shape? If you could touch it what would it feel like? Does it feel warm, cold, or hot? Breathe into it. It can be scary I know. Just go with it. Trust it. Let it radiate. Open up your energy.

Can you think of a time you might have felt this before? It is okay if you haven't. Now fill your body with healing energy. Feel it like liquid from the bottom of your toes. Let this flow up to each part of your body. Move to your ankles, then up to your knees. Move to your hips, your sacred chakra, then up to your belly. Then up to your heart. Now your chest, fill it up, all the way to your shoulders. Down your arms, fill your elbows, wrists and fingers. Then up to your neck, to your face, your nose, your chin, your cheekbones, your forehead. Let it flow to your third eye, let it radiate out the top of your head. Be overflowing with love.

When you are overflowing you have so much more to give. When you pour from your own cup and never fill it back up, you feel drained. Feel it overflowing, know this is love. You are overflowing into the universe. Your love can touch so many. It can pour and nourish the drought. It quenches the thirst. It is amazing. It is powerful. Let yourself be the water. Travel where you want to go. See what path is calling you, what adventure you want to take. There are endless possibilities. It is time to just fly. Just flow, feel the freedom of choice. You are never stuck. Sure, there have been obstacles in your path. Water is powerful, it always finds a way. This is my message. I hope you hear it. You are never alone. We are the drops of water in the ocean of earth.

The words of God are pouring from me. I hear you, I feel you, I am you. There are more possibilities — more than this lifetime can know. It is part of the path, on Earth, that is. It never ends. Of course, we see familiar "drops," old souls, old friends. It is more than that, even this sweater I wear, the computer I am typing on. Shoot, the book you are reading was made with water. So here we are together again. I feel you, do you feel me? I am with you. I am always here. I am always with you. Feel the love. Feel it, Believe it!

Even the gun that took my husband Tim's life was made with water. If he could have known he was never alone. I understand, that was his path. It took a long time to trust it, accept it. I just hope that when you feel alone and want to end the pain, that you drink some water, touch it, feel it. Remember I am with you. We are with you. Feel this book in your hand. Feel your phone or your tablet. Feel it. Touch it. Know I am here. Feel your family, feel your friends. Feel it. Feel the love, let it in. It is true. You are not a drop, you are the ocean. You are the stream. You are the raindrops. You are the swimming pool. You are the beads on your skin when you get out of the shower. That is me, that is you, that is all of us. Water does not die, it merely transforms. It takes a new journey every moment of the day. That is you. It is all of your pain, all of your joy, all of your changes. Yes, sometimes it hurts, deep like a glacier. It boils when you feel anger. That is okay, just let yourself feel it. Just embrace it, follow your path. It is the steam or the pasta nourishing your body.

It never ends, it just changes. Just like our souls. When you lose someone, know you will see them again. When you can, think of the path of one tiny drop. It is incredible. Of course we cannot do it alone. The images keep coming. I see trees, I see flowers, the rain and the sea. I see snow, and the river, the dew on a leaf. I see icicles, ice cubes, a pot full of pasta. The steam rising, clearing your lungs out. I see water in Guatemala that is not very clean. We get dirty and sick and carry it around. We release it, get filtered through mountains and springs. It is an infinite cycle. We all get dirty, we all get sick. We cleanse, we refresh, we feel pure again. God is in you, God is in me. I am you. You are me. We are love. We are connected. I am part of each and every one of you.

Hold your phone in your hand. Feel the couch or the chair that is holding you up. It is all of us. All water, all love. Feel the tears coming down when you finally let me in. When you finally realize I speak the truth. I am right here. I am with you, we all are.

TRANSFORMATION

That is it, the only thing certain is change. It is safe. It was draining and painful to write my story. I wanted to write a fiction novel, with love triangles and maybe some vampires. This book is not what I thought it would be. It is okay to be tired. It keeps the left brain out. It is a story, don't worry, a Creative Non-Fiction. It is a story of healing, of triumph, of deep pain and sorrow. It is a story of adventure, embracing the unknown, but most of all finding joy. You are just letting it unfold, letting it become the tapestry. It is beautiful, it is powerful. It is amazing. Is this resistance? Yes, your body does not want to feel the trauma again. Writing it is draining and exhausting. How did you live that way? You have so much support now, so much love and affection. You do not have to work so hard, but you still do. It is okay to just be you.

I finally get it, I feel it. I am not just a person. I am energy. I am transformation. I am water. My journey has been steady, yet very fast at times. It has been shocking and jarring, or smooth as glass. My fingers are dancing right now, I really feel it coming. I am the water. Flowing and flowing. A story of healing, of spiritual knowing. I had been in a rut, feeling like there was no way out. But, then like a drop dripping and dripping. I found my own path to healing. I made a path where there was not one before. I made it happen, I drifted ashore. I changed direction like salmon upstream. I caused a river, a flood, it would seem.

STORY OF HEALING

As a kid, I was always so afraid. I was so shy and bashful, I hid. When I learned to swim I loved the water. It was so freeing. I loved the sound of ocean waves. I would dream of it and feel it when I slept. I remember sleeping and swaying, swaying to the waves, the ocean in my head.

The first time I swam past the strong waves in the ocean I felt such peace. I had always stayed near the shore, where the waves knock you down. I swam through waves, kicking and struggling past the current until it was calm. Then I swayed with the swell to the rhythm of the sea. It was serene, it was tranquil. I felt the warmth of the sun on my face. It was a loving embrace. I felt peace, I felt hope, I felt love. I felt God. This is God, this is peace, is all I could think. I felt it so strongly more than I had ever felt it in my life. I felt it more than the churches I went to with family, even more than the Santuario, a small Catholic church in Chimayo, New Mexico. I had always felt the strong presence of God there. But this feeling of peace in the water was so powerful. It vibrated and radiated throughout my entire being. I could taste the salty water on my lips. I could hear the waves crashing near the shore and seagulls in the wind. I was floating, supported by love. Like a sponge I absorbed it. I was parched. I was letting it sink in. It was so powerful, I felt so safe and secure. So connected. I returned to that spot again and again I loved it so much. I have tried to return as often as I could, but I live in the desert, it is not as easy as I would like. Before this I had never gotten in all the way. But now, I surrendered. I felt it; my ego was out of the way. I felt God, I felt it, the love in the water, the love inside me.

Let it go, let it go! I just want to sing. I am writing a book about water, I scream. A book about water some people say? I wonder? I wonder what you have to say. I don't know, I say. It is God, not me. God is rhyming in rhythm, words are pouring out like a stream. Who is writing these words, the divine spirit within me? My loving husband Craig pops into my mind. With his gorgeous green eyes that can see deep in my soul. Those eyes that know we have loved each other from long, long ago. Our souls are connected, we chose this you see. To meet up again, in this lifetime. With these children, these parents, these sisters and friends. My daughter, my brown almond-eyed beauty; she dances in my head. She is a character, my love, my old soul. She has been here before, this too I know. She told me as she got out of the car, "Make me a character, put me in your book." I laughed and smiled, well love, here you are. You are in my book.

I feel pouring, dancing from my fingertips. This book about water, it is more than you think. It is more than you know. Follow the direction, with rhythm and flow. It is not for you, or for him, or for her. It is for all of us. For the children, adolescents, adults, our children within. It is a story older than time. It is a story with rhythm and rhyme. Just let it flow, stop trying to stop it. God is the author. Remember the Divine Author within. Trust it. He/she knows what to do. God knows the book, and how to get it outside of you. It is inside, you have heard it before. God wants me to write a book, I kept saying. I had a calling to write. I did not understand, I have never felt like an author. But, I felt like I had to, it was calling my name. Well, here it is. It presented itself. God is writing, it is coming out.

That is the start of each story told, a drop of water. That is how it starts, a journey, a path, the rollercoaster drop. Waves crashing, whales laughing, birds singing and flapping. It is so silly I love it. Now I see the coral reef, like the movie "The Little Mermaid," singing and laughing. I am just wondering, how this is coming from me? What do I know? I don't live near the sea. I live in the desert. I don't get in the water all that much, other than showers and baths and such.

Oh my! Oh dear God, I can't seem to help it. It just keeps coming out in rhyme. It is good, it is silly, it is you. This is the word of God, the Holy Spirit, like Holy Water. It is a story of healing, of grief, of laughter, of joy. It is adventure and sadness and loss. It is New Mexico, Kenya, Africa, all of it. It is the ocean, the river, the hot cocoa. The lavender bubble bath, the smell of the rain. It is me, it is you, it is all the same. It is time for release, time for flow. Just keep going, please just trust it, just let it go. It is ok if it doesn't make sense. It is not supposed to, this is bigger than you. It is bigger than, wider than, a room with a view. It is just a glimpse of what I've been saying.

It is a story of healing that much you know. Is the drop of water a boy or a girl? It is not either, that is the thing. It is both, it is everything. So many of us struggle with limits and lines. Am I a boy or a girl? Do I love boys or girls? How about we all love each other? We are love. You are love. I am love. I love him and her, we are one and the same. We absorb in each other. We love and we hope. We are the passenger in this journey. I like being the passenger of a car when my husband drives. I feel more relaxed. I feel safe, I don't have to be in control. I can trust we are going where we need to, and trust we will get there safely. I can just close my eyes and let it happen. Trust that the genius of the dark night of the soul is to learn how to experience life in a whole new way. It is to help us reveal who we really are, and live a life of passion and purpose. It is finding your calling, and having the courage to listen to your soul. It is happening now. I am just the passenger of this book. It is God writing through me. I am letting the words flow out of me. I am just the vessel.

Our emotions, we have so many, one drop at a time and yet all at once. Relax, you are just letting your body get in the way of what your soul has to say. God chose you, or you volunteered as a soul before you came here. You chose to tell this story, to go on this adventure, to share it. To share what you learned. You are the teacher after all. The teacher, your neighbor Mrs. Watt, more like a grandma, always said you would be. This will teach people. It will show them how to grieve, how to grow, how to heal. How to feel their feelings and let them flow.

Fly with the angels and butterflies. See the world. Float to the clouds in your golden bubble. Visit the fairies, your friends, your sparkling angels. Smile. See the maps all laid out. You are on the adventure, you are on the risky path. You could lose your job, or you could be a millionaire.

El Santuario de Chimayo in Chimayo, New Mexico

Fort Lauderdale Beach, Florida

GAME OF LIFE

This is my baby. I am birthing right now. It does feel like contractions, that is true. I am contracting right now, it is not comfortable, but part of the process. In the process of growth, it can be so uncomfortable. Dark and scary, like the butterfly in the cocoon. Let yourself heal — just rest, you will be out soon. I am so happy, yet confused. My left brain does not know what to do. The part that is an engineer is so puzzled. I just giggle, my angels sing with me. They know the joke. This is fun, so raw, and so real. It is hard to believe, it is truly surreal. I cannot seem to stop it. It is bursting right out of me. Just keep writing, you are almost done. Just keep birthing and birthing this is the one. It is a best seller, New York Times here I come! I'm the next JK Rowling, so much glory, so much fun. I just want to laugh, it is so silly I can't believe it. How is this possible? I just don't know. What in the world do I do? Your words are your voice. A beacon of hope. What a trip to have a book in rhyme. A sing-song book. I never dreamed of it. Just go with it. This is healing. Just keep on breathing, keep on singing. God is in you, in your love. I am love. Let the energy flow, it is from above. You did it! They cry, you did it! They scream. I am so proud of you! Keep going! Those are my angels. Thank you so much. I am so very grateful to you. It is time to write this book. It is my story what can I say? It is your story too. It is all of our stories. We are all connected. That is the point.

The game of life, what a concept. Feathers fluttering. I am delirious. There is so much more to say. It is incredible how this is happening. I am impressed. I am happy. I am so carefree. It was so fun to rhyme. I really loved it. I feel incredibly excited. Thank you, thank you, thank you God. I am so grateful. I need to nourish my body that carries my soul. Not the other way around. God is great, God is good, just write. Let it flow, let it go, can't hold it back anymore. Let it go, let it flow, open the door, the cold never bothered me anyway. Ha, I'm singing now? Breaking out in a "Frozen" song? See, this is fun. The book is unfolding, it is growing.

Let it flow, the drop, the stream, the river, the bounty, the water boiled clean. It is awesome to write about water, it is over the top. Just heal, just feel. Just let it flow, emotions like water are meant to change. That is it, that is the key. Water, like emotions, flowing, transforming. Feel them, do not freeze them, just allow them to happen. Let them go down the stream and flow with the leaf. It is so nice, so relaxing so happy to know. We can go from the top of a leaf to the deepest ocean miles deep.

I have to release it. I hope the message helps. Get it all out so the book can come clearly and without any doubt. Just go for it. Pray for it. Fly to the moon. It will be a success, a best-seller, you know it. Your heart is ready, you feel it, just go for it. I am an author of love, of healing. This book is creative, that I know. It is healing, it touches more than you know. There is so much to the story of me. My adventures, my support, my love to heal. I have had dark moments for sure. So much pain I thought I could not endure. I got through it somehow through God's grace.

At the time I did not acknowledge it, but it was always God. Water always led me to You. My road has been twisted and windy, straight at times, but it always flows to the ocean, to all of God's grace. Was I a mermaid in another life? Who knows? It is hard to say. I am ready God, just keep flowing. The light, the sun, the sound of water flowing. The peacefulness of it. Aah, so relaxing, just keep going.

This is about God, therefore about me. Like the universe, I am part of you. This story is about you, too. It is about all of us. Every single one of us. Each one of us is a part of the vast ocean. We think we are a drop, we feel so alone. The truth is we just keep flowing together, we think we separate or dissolve like steam in the air. Then we turn into clouds and rain everywhere. This is so nice, having so much fun just writing and rhyming. You are releasing, you are healing. You are growing. I like to believe with all my heart, there are no mistakes, just lessons to be learned. I think we never stop growing, not even in death. Our soul just takes on new journeys, new ways to learn. We like to come back and see what else we can learn from this life, these bodies, this planet. I see a whale, an old friend. I keep seeing his eyes, his smile, so familiar, so encouraging. I feel peaceful knowing I am not alone. I am not alone, we are never alone. We must keep going.

Water is healing, water is feeling. What are you feeling? Unsure, cautious, not ready to drop. Just jump in, it is fun. Dive in! We are all here, all your soul mates, angels, and friends far and near. Yes, they are soul mates, and yes, they are angels. So grateful to have them, to have known them. Writing with this rhythm is easier than you think. I always had a hard time thinking I could write like a poet. It just keeps going, it keeps flowing, I know it. The magic, the magic to rhyme. So weird, so strange, writing in rhyme.

Is there evil in water? Some would say yes, those that are afraid. The fear of drowning I suppose, the shock of the water? We are learning to swim, to feel our emotions. It is work, it is hard. We make ourselves numb. It is hard to explain. A coloring book with words of the same. I am safe, I am good, I am kind. Good words, like water to nourish and shine. Replenish, refresh, let it all go. What happens next, the drop says to the pool?

Just jump in, go with it. Be the child jumping in, full of joy. Be free, without a care in the world. I want to be that child. I do. I want to see my soul happy too. This could be a coloring book. For grownups and children that want to heal. Coloring, with rhythms, so brilliant! The want, the desire to heal.

I get it now, I am Oprah, Louise Hay. Who knew it was possible? It is true. I am here, you are here, let's do it. When you think of water what do you see? A cup, a lake, an ocean, a pool? There is no right answer. Just remember, you are beautiful, you are worthy, you are good, you are kind. You are lovely and beautiful, more than your mind. That is what the words of water want to say. They want to flow, to sing, to go all the way. Water is magic. Magic is love. Manifest it and get it, love from above. It's time to start healing, let's do it, let's go!

This is the path to hope, to love, change and healing. To remember the choice. We often choose to think we are all alone, the single drop. It is hard to remember we are part of the big ocean, the earth made of water. We can choose to think differently. That is the key, the way out of depression. It is easier to think negatively and slide down that slippery slope. It comes fast if you let it, the sadness, the fear, anxiety, resistance. It is hard to think differently, but we can choose to. Let yourself think of love, of joy, and of peace. There is always a choice in the flow. We do not disappear, we keep going and going, ever changing and growing.

NOAH'S ARK

I love you so much, my children. All of you, I want you to heal. Clean the world, lighten your soul. A metaphor for Noah's ark. Was the earth really covered in water to heal and cleanse? A metaphor for using any water, we know. So lucky we are to have access to water all times of the day. From the sink, to the toilet, to water bottles, to rain. So let us use it to cleanse ourselves, to start over again. We do not have to get on a boat. Just remember. It is all part of the plan, we are healing, always healing; just let it go.

A divining rod used to find water. Our path, our journey, it is our divining rod. It is our road to creativity, to love. The passageway to good feelings, to sad feelings, emotion. The scary feelings too. With the tears and the heartache, fear of the unknown. It can be so very scary to some. To trust we are safe.

The power of healing, of water, so revealing. Our trauma, our pain that we carry around. Water is healing. Get in the water with someone you love and hold dear. Remember the relationship is clear. Just keep going, keep flowing. God is with you, inside you, you are God, you are love. I am love. I am the drop, I move and I flow. I go up the stem, I make the petal grow. I shift and I waver, then absorb and go down.

Just relax. Just enjoy it. I can do Zen tangles. I can make them like waves. Oh my God, this is awesome. I am so happy, so ready! Cool beans! I am an author, a writer of books. That is crazy, so crazy I feel like a kook! Your story was needed for it to keep going. Your story of healing and growing. You learn from the past, you look forward to the future. You are magic, you can conjure it. Make it appear.

That is life! Your thoughts, the path, are part of the drop. To the ocean and rivers, it never stops. I keep going and going in circles with it. Perhaps because it never ends. It keeps going and going and changing. I am this drop of water. I am the ocean, I am the river, I am the stream, I am the swimming pool, I am the boiling water, I am the ice. I am.

This knowledge will help us heal. It helps us find meaning, find peace in the everyday quest. Understanding the journey is healing. Understanding that pain and turmoil are part of the process. Live your life, just keep going. Now you know, you cannot deny it. You are never ever alone. Not for a second, never at all. We are all like this tiny drop. Moving, dripping, holding on to the bottle with all of our might. We fear what will happen, so afraid of the unknown. Witches and fairies and magical creatures. Things we cannot see. Like electricity.

Water is something we can all understand. We see it, we feel it, touch it with our hand. It changes when pure, it changes with color, just like feelings, just like waves. Yes, it heals. Jump in, feel whole, shake it up. Do not be afraid.

A book of healing, of water. A story of growing and learning to love, to remember we connected long, long ago. This love is great, this love is healing. I think of my husband and his beautiful green eyes, my daughter's like almonds, deep and wise. These words are powerful. A beacon of light, a beacon of hope I have a connection. I feel like the Pope!

Ha! I too have a direct line with God. I feel it, I am it. It is true, here it comes. These words are not mine, they are God's. I feel it, I just keep hoping, and seeing, and believing. Thank you God, thank you Lord for this day. For letting me feel you and hear this way.

It is amazing to rhyme like this. I feel your son in my heart. I feel like singing, I am hearing a harp. I feel you strongly, like I do in the ocean. Thank you God, thank you. This book is part you and part me. I am inside of You, can't you see. I am everything. You are everything too. We are all of it, every part of it. The ocean is calling my name. I want to feel it, submerge in it. That sounds so lovely.

I just cannot seem to get over it, to be writing in rhythm. I am trying to trust it, not deny it. It is God, yet it is me. A poet, an artist. I paint, I play, I heal with my words, why not through poetry? How silly of me to have doubted. Of course you can heal with words. You do it every day. You heal, you feel, you know what to say. No, it does not come out in rhyme, it was so you could see. You can be playful, have fun, just be silly. You can be healing, and funny, and creative as hell. Oh my Goddess, you are funny, too funny. So silly, so crazy it just will not stop. The magic, the words, the pouring of the heart. It beats like the drum to its own rhythm, just like my heart. Not consistent, but lovely and beautiful too. I am so happy to find my way through.

Thank you, thank you, thank you God, for this magical day. I am not alone. I never was and never will be. It took you making a poet out of me. I feel my life has transformed. The life I want is about to be born. I will be free to be me. I will have more time to relax, love my children. I will enjoy the laughter, the times when they glow. I can see them learn, see them fumble, see them grow.

That must be how it feels to watch me. A light bulb went off today. Thank you God, what else can I say? I am so happy to be here, so happy to write. To release the past, to have joy, and delight. I could dance, I could sing, twirl and spin. I feel like a kid. Spinning and spinning. I just want to boogie and see myself grinning. This is really cracking me up. I keep laughing at myself. How can a book of rhyming be coming from me?

I feel so creative, like a painter with words. Painting the landscape and beautiful birds. The flowers are bursting with color, the sparkle in the eye of soul. It is time, it is your mural, your painting of feeling. Just go with it. Paint it, let the colors flow with the music of it. Just go with it. No lines to stop you. Just keep going, keep going, keep flowing, and growing. It is time. It is time to know.

You are an angel. An angel right now. Oh no, I think, I am too wicked, dark and gloomy. I hear a chuckle. You heal, you paint, you create. You are already an angel to many. More than you know. You are ready, you are ready for this, get it going. I am distracted from the noise and the questions. I hear the doubt in my head, the fear in my heart, push it out, push it out. Radiate God, shine, bright light. Push out all doubt. I will publish this book. I will get it out there. These are God's words, not mine. It is the calling I felt to write this book. This is a book of love, of hope, of fun. A book for my family, my beautiful family of earth. All my children, all my creatures, all of the growth. Thank you God. Thank you so much for choosing me to

let this come out. Thank you for my blessings.
Thank you for the ones still coming.

BEYOND THE SENSES

Water, take me away. Fizzle and gurgle, change and adapt. Heat up, dissipate, freeze, never-ending possibilities. It is endless, limitless. Water has no limits. We try to control it, make it flow a certain way, but really it will go how it is supposed to. Let it flow, let it change. Embrace it. Honor it, smell it, touch it, feel it, taste it, hear it. Go beyond the senses; smell, touch, taste, sound, visual. Taste: sour, bitter, refreshing, soothing. I am everything. The sound of raindrops, crashing waves, wet and gooey. The smell of rain, the smell of salt water, the smell of the ocean, a lake, or a shower. The steam, or the brisk, fresh smell of new snow. The scent of ice, even the smell of boiling water. It is the sparkle of frost in the morning. Beyond that it is the infinite, never-ending flow of life. Let it flow. Trust the water knows where to go. The adventure, never-ending adventures. So many transformations, so many possibilities. Truly, dazzling crystals, to deep blue oceans, to savory soup. My very own chicken soup of the soul. Water, healing the soul. The soul connected to water. The soul is a drop of water choosing different journeys, different paths, a continuous cycle. Tingles, shivers, the power of water. The connection to our soul. The journey we choose to take, the paths to the unknown, scarce or abundant. Flowing nonstop or springing one drop at a time from the earth. Making its way to a new journey.

We are all on journeys. There is no I, we are love, we are water. We search for water throughout the universe. Did we travel to this, did we leave other planets, are we in different forms? A form beyond this, beyond our little comprehension? There is so much we do not know. Our little hearts flow, connect to me God, breathe into me, let it go and flow and flow. The honey and lemon, warm water so soothing and cleansing. A drop of water or the entire ocean. It is hard to say, I am really both. It goes, it connects. It breathes like a fish breathes under water. Was I a mermaid, a magical creature? I am flowing through the soul. The water of the soul. I feel God. I am God. I love all souls. I see people's souls, the exterior is just the shape the water formed into. Like an ice cube in a mold. I am God, a fraction, a fractal, a molecule of water, shifting and changing. I am God, flowing. I am a drop of a water, I am the coyote, the tree, the roots, the water that made this paper, the mold for this pen, the ink, the plastic, the wood. I am everywhere. I am water. I am God. Flow through me, pour the words out of me. The words are flowing like a stream into the ocean. Connect, be in the water. Be embraced. Be completely submerged. Feel it completely around you, comforting, seeping into your pores. It is you, I am you. It flows together. We are all attached. I am the fish, the coral, the mermaid, the shark. I am the tiger, the ocean, the waterfall, the owl, the eagle, the hawk. I am. Let it flow. I am everything. We can never be alone. We are thoughts, we are in constant flow.

My left brain is trying to tell me what to do. It says this does not make any sense and I should just stop. I am trying to trust these words to flow out. I just have to trust the process, go into my heart. I open my soul, open the tunnel of light. I let the divine energy flow through.

FORGIVENESS

I have forgiven Tim. At times I still get angry, but mostly sad that he is missing out on seeing the amazing things our children do. They are so talented, gifted, and giving. Forgiveness was at times a difficult process. I had to forgive him for several things. Every time I would believe I had completely forgiven him, something new would come up and I would be angry again. But honestly, the hardest thing of all was learning how to forgive myself.

I held onto guilt for a long time. I had to learn how to be kind to myself, to love myself. I now accept that I sometimes cry inappropriately. I sometimes get triggered by the weirdest things. Like seeing SpongeBob (Tim loved SpongeBob Squarepants) or dolphins, (Lori's favorite), or when I got my first set of checks with my name only on it. People have tried to help or have given advice.

Everyone grieves in their own way. There is no right way. The best thing to do for someone that is grieving is to listen. Just be there and listen. That's it. Sometimes we just need our pain to be acknowledged. Learning this did not come easy. It has taken years of therapy and the Children's Grief Center of New Mexico to let it sink in.

In the process of forgiving Tim, I learned to thank him. I deeply appreciate the time we had together. Angels come in many forms. They guide us and teach us. Sometimes they must get our attention through drastic measures. The lesson he taught me was how to love myself. I sometimes think that as an angel walking the earth, he could not bear the pain he felt here and longed to go home. I have a better understanding of those dark desperate suicidal moments. Perhaps in the depths of his despair he truly believed the world would be better without him. He must have thought that ending his life would end his suffering. What he did not understand is that it was transferred to us. The extent of his alcoholism was beyond my understanding at the time. In our desperate love for him, we would have continued to accept his disease. Perhaps it was his attempt to force us out of the dysfunction. Through all this speculation, I simply wish he could have experienced what I have. How those dark agonizing nights are part of the transformation towards our best life. If only he had known that he was not alone. It saddens me deeply that he was unable to feel the connection and oneness we all share.

My dearest Timothy, I am forever grateful for your love. I am so thankful for the support I felt and feel from you still. Thank you for the love you gave here on earth. Most of all, thank you forcing me to learn how to love myself.

Now I love my life, I have a private practice as a counselor and play therapist. I am married to my wonderful, supportive husband Craig. I love our family. We are both very close to our parents, siblings, aunts, uncles, cousins and friends. We spend weekends going to birthday parties and family gatherings. I love the little things, the moments we share. I have so much fun going to concerts and cruises with my husband. Moments like going out to breakfast or coffee with my son, hearing him talk about colleges and the future. I love making my oldest daughter laugh when I watch scary movies with her. Memories of listening to my daughter play the violin and watching her smile with pride at doing something new at gymnastics. Having a good laugh when I volunteer at my youngest daughter's elementary school, listening to all the silly things kindergartners say. I look forward to having lunch with my sister and best friend, and enjoying concerts with my nephew. I love having barbeques or impromptu dinners with our parents. We have a family full of laughter and love. Summers are full of swimming and fun trips. I love having a pool. I love to joke that the kids grow gills like fish in the summer. Like me as a child, they would stay in the water all day if we let them.

What I've heard is true. When one door shuts another one opens. I am so thankful for all the doors that have opened for me. It has been remarkable and frankly spectacular. I've had more opportunities than I ever imagined. Thank you, thank you, thank you God. I appreciate how incredibly blessed I am.

SILLY

So be open to love. This is it, let the story unfold. Wasn't it fun to rhyme out of your bones? Whoo! You are an ox! So funny, so frivolous, so crazy! Just keep flowing. The words just pour out. This is so amusing I could laugh. I always stopped myself from letting the words rhyme. But really it is so fun! I am laughing at myself! I am laughing out loud! So silly, so innocent, what a release! I love it.

It is joyous, it is freeing and fun! So leap in, belly flop in the water. Feel it all around you. Submerge yourself in it, scream in it. Laugh as loud as you can. Blow bubbles under water. Yell at the top your lungs under water. Cuss and curse the world if you like. It is safe, you are safe. It is healing.

We heal in relationships, that is what I believe. Well, this is a way to show we are never alone. We are connected. Smile at the next person you see. They are part of you, they are part of this journey. When you take your next drink of water, feel the love of millions. Feel your friends. Feel your partners, your lovers, even your enemies. They are part of this, too.

We are the ocean. We are the sharks. We are the sharks and the turtles and tiger fish. I see my polar bear jumping and playing. Remember to have fun. Be silly! Run through the sprinkler. Have a water fight. Throw a snowball. Jump in the pool, feel alive!

I cannot wait to see you my friends. I will see you soon, Oprah Winfrey, even Joel Olsteen. I never imagined myself thinking this way, yet here I am. I am spreading your message of love. I am. I am. I am. Here it goes: I am water. I am love. I am earth. I am power. I am hope. I am faith. I am joy. Faith, hope, and love, the greatest of these is love.

Joy, my word of the year. This year I did a Documented Faith journal, where you pick a word of the year. Have I really let joy in? At moments, but not nearly enough. I too am afraid if I let it soak in, something bad will come. I fear having my joy taken away. It is okay, it is safe. Let yourself feel it. It is part of the process. It is part of the journey. It is the adventure, the excitement, the unknown. Just let yourself feel it, let it really soak in. Scream it, laugh it. Feel the joy!! Be in love, dance, jump around. Act silly, do cartwheels, dance, be a clown!! Shake like a dog. Howl at the moon! Enjoy it, embrace it. Love this wild water ride.

I hear the crickets, the coyote, I feel the energy. What is the message I really need to hear? Open your heart. Open it up, your back heart too. Thank you coyote. Thank you, beautiful creatures cheering me on. I see dolphins, sharks, and turtles swimming. I hear eagles, seagulls, bluejays and owls. I see tigers, leopards, lions, and lizards. I see lady bugs and butterflies flying out of the cocoon. I am sky diving, snorkeling, and drawing the moon. Draw a picture. Color, be silly, cut paper, and throw it.

Yes I have been hurt and betrayed. I have felt used. Right now I am in love and as happy as ever. But, I too tend to wear myself out. I do not follow my own rules. I too, need more self care. At times I have let that slip and let my fear in. I built up my wall, not letting any love in. I too, am guilty of feeling alone. Or I feel overwhelmed, like I must do everything. Like you, I must work on loving myself. I want to love myself enough to have more fun. To dance and act silly and goofy. To jump like a kid on a large trampoline, to feel ready to fly like you do on a swing.

So live!! Jump in! Feel it! Breathe! Dance! I know you can do it. I cannot do it for you, you have to choose. I can just give you the tools. This book is about healing, you had a feeling. This book will help so many people to heal. Your story of healing helps others to heal, to believe and trust. To have faith and know.

Feel confident, feel powerful, feel beautiful, feel amazing. Feel sexy and smart and like the world is in your hands. Travel countries, climb mountains, jump off cliffs. Ride the waves, swim with dolphins, and snorkel! Do not be afraid. You are safe. If you worry you cannot swim; take a look. You already have. You swam here, you made it. Just like Dory. You know you can. You are safe.

Take a shower, wash your face. It is fine, you are fine. You are safe. You can shine.

There is so much to say I do not know where to begin. It can be tough. Sharing, being vulnerable, I know it. It is scary who wants to get hurt? No one wants to, yet we all do. Every single one of us. We have been hurt in one way or another. We heal, you can heal. You can enjoy life. Just breathe, drink some water. I know you are tired or feeling worn out. Just trust it. If you are tired wash your hands. Feel the water. Feel the love. Remember. We are here, I am here. I love you. You are loved. Water is healing. Water is love.

Touch this book, feel the pages. Feel the energy, feel the love. It was made with water. I love you. I love you. Literally, I, Yvonne, love you so much. God loves you. You are loved, believe it.

Play! Have fun! Jump in! Go for it! Are you ready? Why not? Let's do it. Did you do it? Did you feel it? Wasn't it awesome? I see all my clients. I see their eyes. I see their pain, they are healing, they are letting the words soak in. Writing about this is healing me, it can heal you too.

So now it is your turn, go drink some water. Jump in a lake! Okay, it does not have to be a lake, just some water. This is a powerful message. I believe it will help you heal. Let yourself feel it. Believe it. Really feel it. I am connected to you. You are connected to me. This is about healing and not feeling alone.

I feel the drops of water. I feel it on my skin. I see it start to pour. It rains so hard. It floods the road. It cleanses. It pushes away the dirt. The smell is amazing. The taste is refreshing. I jump in the stream. I drop from a leaf. It takes me on a beautiful journey through yellow leaves and crunchy snow. I feel the freshness of it. It is so peaceful, so stunningly gorgeous.

I am the river full of fish. I am the fishermen sitting on their chairs. They love to sit and just wait for a fish. The water is healing, it is serene and calm. The surfers ride the waves. The dolphins jump through the water. Always back to my friend the whale, who smiles and waves. The top of a mountain covered with snow. I can see the drops turning into a waterfall. Touch a little drop of water. Look at it. Feel it. Imagine you are it. Even if you fall onto the floor and get wiped up with a towel, that towel just absorbed you. You are still not alone. It holds you, embraces you.

Abuse makes us feel dirty whether it is physical, sexual, or emotional. We use water to clean, to try to wash it away. Some people still do not feel clean, like they cannot wash it off. Cold water makes you feel alive. It shocks you. I think I help people get spiritually fed. I hope you feel and get out of your head. I know most of us live in our head. We do not know how to let ourselves feel. It is part of the journey, a part of the process. Does a tingle have to be bad? Does a breeze have to feel scary? Why not nice? Who wants to feel the pain of feeling gross, of feeling dirty, of feeling like there is something wrong with you? Who wants to be afraid of attention? Or fear they will get hurt if they get it? Who likes to downplay their sexuality? Just when they start to like it, they get scared. They go back to putting layers on, whether it is layers of clothes, or layers of fat. It is a layer of protection.

I am no different, I lose weight, I put it on again. I think I have healed from it, yet I do it again and again. It is hard to think about being connected to an abuser. If we are connected, how can we hate our perpetrators? How can I hate anyone if I am connected to them? Then I would hate myself. If I am connected to terrorists how can I love them? They do not believe we are connected. That is the point. If they did, they would not have to destroy. We will all meet up again, like I said, the rain here is the same rain everywhere. That is a tough argument. I know not everyone will agree. That is okay. I believe. I have enough faith for all of us.

I do. I have faith. You will start to believe it. You will have compassion. You will be grateful. Think of the water washing away the blood from a gun or a cut. Water really does heal us all, if you let it. It is up you. You have the choice. I am choosing yes. I am choosing love. I choose to heal. What are you going to choose?

You are loved. I am loved. Say it. I am Love. You have so much to give. You have so much to give to the world. If you could just remember you are part of the plan you are part of the journey. This is it! You are ready!! What do you choose? I choose love, I choose hope.

Sharing my story was needed and important. I too have felt broken. I have struggled, I have hurt. I have had trauma. I have had my share of loss and pain. I have had to keep going, even when I wanted the world to stop. I now understand it is part of the adventure.

Do not be afraid. Just keep going. Think of all the people you have loved. Imagine all the souls you will love still. Hold in your heart all those you have helped heal. This is just the next stop. Where do I go from here? I am not sure. Why did I share some of my story? So I could be vulnerable and real. So you would know I too, have been cut open and raw. Writing this helped me feel the presence of God. I feel it in my soul. Know the power you have right here. The power that is available to us all. The power of a drop of water.

REFERENCES

Bird, Tom. <u>You Can... Write Your Book in a Weekend</u>. Sedona: Sojourn Publishing, 2013.

Cameron, Julia. <u>The Artist's Way, A Spiritual Path to Higher Creativity</u>. New York: Penguin Putnam, 1992.

Cameron, Julia. <u>Finding Water: The Art of Perseverance (Artist's Way)</u>. New York: Jeremy P. Tarcher/Penguin, 2009.

Emoto, Masaru. <u>The Hidden Messages In Water</u>. Hillsboro: Beyond Words Publishing, 2004.

Frankl, Viktor E. <u>Man's Search For Meaning</u>. Verlag fur Jugen und Volk (Austria), 1946. Beacon Press (United States), 1959.

Hay, Louise. <u>You Can Heal Your Life</u>. Santa Monica: Hay House, 1984

Rowling, J.K. <u>Harry Potter and the Chamber of Secrets</u>. New York: Scholastic, 1999.

Shapiro, Francine. <u>Eye Movement Desensitization and Reprocessing, Basic Principles, Protocols, and Procedures, 2nd Edition</u>. New York: Guilford Press, 2001.

OTHER RESOURCES

A.A. (Alcoholics Anonymous) is an international mutual aid fellowship of men and women who have had a drinking problem. It is nonprofessional, self-supporting, multiracial, apolitical, and available almost everywhere. There are no age or education requirements. Membership is open to anyone who wants to do something about his or her drinking problem.

For more information and to find a meeting near you, please visit www.aa.org

Al-Anon and Alateen Family Groups are a fellowship of relatives and friends of alcoholics who share their experience, strength and hope in order to solve their common problems.

For more information and to find a meeting near you, visit http://www.al-anon.alateen.org/

The Children's Grief Center of New Mexico provides a safe and supportive environment for young people (ages 5—25) and their caregivers who have experienced the death of someone significant in their lives. Services are provided at no charge. Donations are gratefully accepted.

For more information and resources please visit http://www.childrensgrief.org/

Children's Grief Center of New Mexico
3001 Trellis Dr. NW
Albuquerque, NM 87107
Phone: (505) 323-0478
info@childrensgrief.org
www.childrensgrief.org

EMDR (Eye Movement Desensitization and Reprocessing) is a psychotherapy that enables people to heal from the symptoms and emotional distress that are the result of disturbing life experiences. Repeated studies show that by using EMDR therapy people can experience the benefits of psychotherapy that once took years to make a difference.

For more information and resources please visit http://www.emdr.com/

The National Alliance for Grieving Children promotes awareness of the needs of children and teens grieving a death and provides education and resources for anyone who wants to support them.

For more information and to find support in your area please visit https://childrengrieve.org/

National Suicide Prevention Lifeline

If you feel you are in a crisis, whether or not you are thinking about killing yourself, please call the National Suicide Prevention Lifeline. People have called for help with substance abuse, economic worries, relationship and family problems, sexual orientation, illness, getting over abuse, depression, mental and physical illness, and even loneliness.

No matter what problems you are dealing with, we want to help you find a reason to keep living. By calling 1-800-273-TALK (8255) you'll be connected to a skilled, trained counselor at a crisis center in your area, **anytime 24/7.**

1-800-273-TALK (8255)

For more information please visit http://www.suicide
preventionlifeline.org/

Another helpful resource on coping with suicide:
http://www.suicidefindinghope.com/

'Write Your Best Seller in a Weekend' Retreat
using The Tom Bird Method

For more information and resources visit
http://tombird.com/

TOM BIRD
#1 Best Selling Author and Literary Shaman
928-821-6946
tombird@tombird.com
TomBird.com

38455645R00123

Made in the USA
San Bernardino, CA
06 September 2016